ZAMBEZI REFLECTIONS

SUSAN RYDING

Zambezi Reflections

Editing and formatting by Let's Get Booked

www.letsgetbooked.com

Cover art and design by Rachel Spelling

www.studiospelling.com

Proofreading by Rachael Prest

www.rachaelprestediting.com

Print ISBN: 978-1-7399193-0-6

eBook ISBN: 978-1-7399193-1-3

Greystone Publishing

For Beck and Esca

I love you

I absolutely loved reading Ryding's stories about teaching in Namibia. Zambezi Reflections provided a unique, often funny, insight into her experience. Ryding is clearly a warm hearted person and, in turn, has been taken into the hearts of her colleagues, friends and neighbours in Chinchimane.

Sarah Gorman

Susan Ryding's memories of her time teaching in Namibia are often funny, occasionally sad, and always warm and honest. Her wry humour and self-awareness make her a delightful narrator as she takes you with her on a leap into the unknown.

Rachael Prest

CHAPTER 1
IN THE BEGINNING

A leap of hope. A leap of faith. A leap into the unknown.

It is an arduous task to pack for a twenty-seven-month trip to a place you know little about. I was moving to Chinchimane, a remote village in north east Namibia, 60km from the nearest town and with no running water or electricity. I had been advised to pack mementoes to combat homesickness: photographs and books, lots of books. Apparently, book shops were scarce in Namibia and books expensive. I packed a few clothes, a pair of sturdy sandals, a Tilly hat and a pac a mac for the rainy season. Friends asked whether I felt nervous about moving to Namibia. Was I worried about getting ill or getting lost or facing traumatic situations far from family and friends? I didn't allow myself to think too much about what my life might be like over there; too much fretting, too much thinking, and I probably wouldn't go. I based my knowledge of African countries on media coverage of horrific civil wars, child soldiers, AIDS and famine. The news we receive from Africa is often negative and while I knew that this would not be the full story, I really did not know what to expect.

What was I worried about? Honestly? I am embarrassed to admit that I was superficially preoccupied with the ridiculously trivial. Losing my tweezers and not being able to buy any more out in the village; the increasing numbers of random chin and neck hairs I sprout, seemingly overnight, would get out of control. I worried about hairy legs. What if I couldn't get razors? Did Namibian women shave their legs? What if I couldn't get anti-dandruff shampoo over there? How many bottles of Head & Shoulders could I fit in my luggage? Would I be able to buy contact lens solution, or would I need to wear my specs all the time? What if I broke them? When you see photographs of people off on their travels, exploring and having wild adventures, they look lustrous and tanned and smooth. Two years was a long time, and I was in danger of ending up hairy and bearded, sprinkled with dandruff, my specs held together with Sellotape. If I was struggling to find Mr Right with the whole of Boots at my disposal, prospects did not look good marooned in the African bush. I am ashamed of my shallow vanity, but these are genuinely the issues that preyed on my mind – until the second I arrived in Windhoek, that is. Glossy, beautiful, capital city Windhoek where you could buy anything you might possibly need. I ate sushi and drank prosecco in the shopping mall, and I bought spare tweezers and pink razors, lip gloss and dangly earrings.

Let's backtrack twelve months; I was twenty-nine years old, a restless age where people seem to make moves to settle down or realise they have some exploring to do. Most of my friends were in serious relationships, starting to talk about marriage and babies. Mortgages were discussed, pensions set up, and sensible, inevitable maturity beckoned. I was a science teacher, recently single and feeling left out of settling-down conversations. I was desperate to live abroad, and I didn't really mind where. I was too lacking in confidence and savings to simply pack my bags and head off to see the world. I didn't crave a backpacking tour; I wanted to make a new home and true friends. I was looking for a teaching job somewhere, but not in a private school, and I only speak English. The job pages of the Times Educational Supplement were bursting with amazing overseas vacancies, but they were restricted to private international schools.

My options seemed rather limited until I heard about Voluntary Service Overseas (VSO). I was initially put off by the word "voluntary"; I needed an income, plus volunteering sounded a little too earnest. Research revealed that I would receive training, flights, a living wage and a place to live. I am sure many people embark on VSO for entirely altruistic reasons. I am afraid I did not; I was itching for an adventure and desperate to get away. I did some further research and with rising excitement read that there were many vacancies for education posts in Papua New Guinea and Vanuatu in the South Pacific. I had never seen the Pacific Ocean (still haven't), and I started to feel that this was the answer I was looking for. I read *The Lost Tribe* by Edward Marriott and images of white sand, and warm, turquoise waters drifted into my head. Perhaps my classroom would be a grass-roofed hut on the beach. These fantasies were extinguished when I spoke to someone at VSO, no single women were currently being sent to Papua New Guinea on account of a string of sexual assaults, and their programme in Vanuatu had finished; all of their education posts were now based in Africa. I took *The Lost Tribe* back to the library and borrowed Paul Theroux's *Dark Star Safari* instead.

I sent off an application form and was invited to attend an interview in London. The interview was fun, and I met lots of interesting people. One group task involved taking turns to name the guilty pleasures we might miss. The first person said imported Alphonso mangoes and Montezuma's chocolate; I quickly changed my guilty pleasure to something a little more middle class. The interview was followed by a matching process, where individuals' skills and expertise were coordinated with a country's requirements. VSO education programmes were offered alongside jobs relating to secure livelihoods, health, conservation and local governance. I filled in a form stating my preference for where I would like to live. I indicated a rural location – a remote village sounded more romantic. I wanted a community of my own, uncluttered by other volunteers and ex-pat social circles, although in the end it was these that helped keep me afloat. All the options I was given were positions for a physical science teacher trainer, combining classroom teaching with resource development and support for other science teachers from surrounding schools. The first vacancy was for a single-year placement in Zambia, the second a twenty-seven-month contract in Eritrea and the third in Namibia. I ruled out Zambia as every returned volunteer I spoke to said that you spend the first year finding your feet and learning; it was only in the second year that they felt their work had any long-term impact. The Eritrean job was in a devout Muslim area, and I was pretty sure that this would not sit well with my penchant for boozy nights out.

That left Namibia, which I am embarrassed to say I had never heard of. Here in the UK, we now know Namibia because of its growing tourist trade, photogenic sand dunes and World Cup-qualifying rugby team, but all those years ago it wasn't on my radar. I looked it up in an atlas; Namibia sits just above South Africa on the west of the continent, and it is huge – 825,615km^2. That is over three times the size of the UK. The school where I would be working was in a small village called Chinchimane in the far north east of the country, 60km along a gravel road from the nearest town of any size. The town, Katima Mulilo, was described in my guidebook as "something of a wild west frontier town".

This was starting to sound promising. Apparently, the head teacher from the school in Chinchimane, Mrs Mahoto, had requested a volunteer science teacher three years ago but VSO could not fill the post, possibly due to its remote location and the lack of electricity or running water in the village. Feeling somewhat reckless, I ticked the Namibia box, handed in my notice at work and turned my thoughts to packing.

I arrived in Windhoek on 11th September 2006 along with twenty other volunteers. Unfortunately, due to a baggage handling cock up my thoughtfully packed rucksack remained at Manchester airport for three days. I made immediate and long-lasting friendships as I had to borrow knickers, clothes and toiletries. We were a mixed bunch from the UK, Ireland, the Philippines, the Netherlands, Kenya and Uganda. Most of our group were at the beginning or end of our careers, in our late twenties and early thirties or recently retired. There was an even mix of couples and single folk, although a few had left partners at home (evidently a recipe for infidelity); the women outnumbered the men by three to one.

Members of our group would be working as teachers, occupational therapists, accountants, IT consultants, health professionals, fundraisers and wildlife rangers. The brilliant thing about VSO is that it involves well-qualified, experienced professionals, neatly matched to the needs of the country that has requested them. There is welcome debate about the negative side of overseas volunteering (voluntourism), where inexperienced people sign up for short-term projects that have little long-term positive impact. Many young people have the well-meaning desire to work in an orphanage or build a school as part of their gap year, but young children, especially those with no family, require stability, not a steady stream of nervous fresh faces every few months. The message is clear: do some research, make sure that you will not be the only one who benefits from your volunteering experience, and above all make sure it isn't actually doing harm, as with orphanage volunteering programmes.

VSO attempted to match one country's strengths with areas of need in another to ensure sustainability and constructive impact. For example, Uganda, like the rest of sub-Saharan Africa, is in the grip of an AIDS epidemic and during the 1980s and early 1990s HIV infection rates were at 30%. In 1992, a national HIV/AIDS policy was developed in Uganda, widely regarded as the most effective national response to the disease as infection rates fell to 6.4%. So, VSO sent volunteers from Uganda to help Namibians tackle their own growing HIV crisis (when I moved there, 43% of pregnant women in the Zambezi Region of Namibia were HIV-positive). English language teachers were sent from the Netherlands and wildlife conservation experts from Kenya. The UK education system is respected internationally (I wonder will that continue as our class sizes grow and teachers become ever more stretched and stressed) and most of the education professionals were Brits.

We were a friendly bunch and those first two weeks brimmed with excitement and easy laughter. We had health and safety training and a brief introduction to the history of the regions we would be moving to. My favourite bit was when we learnt about different snakes, how to recognise the venomous ones and how to avoid getting bitten. I will pass on two remembered pieces of advice which may be useful one day: if you see a dead snake don't poke it with a stick, it may not be dead, but you soon could be; and don't pose for a photograph next to a termite mound – abandoned mounds are a favourite nesting site for the dreaded black mamba (killer rating 89 in predator Top Trumps, venom lethal within twenty minutes). We got our own HIV awareness and prevention talk based on the assumption of "when, not if" we would be having sex during our placement and we were all issued with free condoms. One of the Kenyan volunteers demonstrated this to be ineffective by getting a local woman pregnant within a few months of arriving. However, the couple is still together, and as I type this, his daughter has just turned sixteen.

We split up into groups for introductory language training. There are around thirty different languages spoken in Namibia; for a country with such a low population it is incredibly culturally and linguistically diverse. In the Zambezi Region where I would be living there are five languages in regular use. We were told that most people were fluent in at least three different languages and that since independence in 1990, English has replaced Afrikaans as the lingua franca. Five of us would be living in or around Katima Mulilo, and we were taught some basic Silozi language phrases by a young woman called Emily: *Mutozi* (good day), *tsamay hande* (go well), *ni tumezi* (thank you) and *mulikani* (please) are about all I can remember. Over the two years, I got fairly good at listening and getting the general gist of a conversation, usually from the smattering of English words dropped into it, but my spoken Silozi was appalling. I could wheel out a few crowd-pleasing phrases from time to time for politeness or amusement, but I am afraid my grasp of the local language was typically British. The Namibians I worked with could skip between English, Silozi and Subeya (two of the most common local languages in our village) without pausing for breath; many had a fourth language too. How many English people could even say "good morning" to our Welsh neighbours in their own language?

During that induction fortnight, we had the chance to head into the city and buy anything we might need before moving to more remote areas. I bought clothes, a guide to the wildlife of Namibia and a small two-man tent.

A few volunteers were to be based in Windhoek, but most of us had jobs in the north. After two weeks of feeling like I was on an exciting holiday, the real adventure was about to begin. We set off together in a fleet of shared lifts, gradually saying goodbye and peeling off to our new homes. Those of us heading to Katima Mulilo had the longest journey – 1,226km in total. We got a lift as far as Rundu, a medium-sized town separated from Angola by the Okavango River. As we got further from Windhoek, the landscape became wilder and the settlements more ramshackle. We spent the night in Rundu before getting another lift for the final five-hour road trip to Katima Mulilo. In 2000, a military escort system was set up on the 212km stretch of road between Bagani and Kongola, with two convoys leaving in each direction every day. There had been a series of ambushes attributed to UNITA[1] rebels. Seven people were shot and killed in the space of three weeks and many more injured in grenade and assault rifle attacks. The deaths of two French children made international headlines and threatened the burgeoning tourist industry. Thankfully, the region has been peaceful for many years now, and the escort was suspended in 2002.

I shared a car with Addie and Barbara, retired physics and maths teachers from Bury. Barbara gave birth to her eldest son on the same maternity ward where Mum gave birth to me (the Sharoe Green hospital in Preston, long

---

[1] National Union for the Total Independence of Angola

since demolished). He was born two days after me while I was still on the ward, so technically, Barbara and I had already met. I wonder if that is why we hit it off straight away. I really enjoyed their company; we are all missing out hugely if we only select friends from within our own age group. In the car ahead were a married couple my age who had been incredibly organised and already bought their own car while in Windhoek. Two hours into the journey, while passing through the Mudumu National Park, we saw a group of elephants grazing at the side of the road. We stopped to take photographs; I still felt like I was on holiday.

As we approached Katima Mulilo, nerves finally began to kick in; this was going to be my town, my turf for the next two years. First impressions were that it was a bit of a dump. Shrubby vegetation at the side of the road was festooned with litter and plastic bags, a couple of concrete shops and bars looked abandoned, and the settlements we encountered were dilapidated. I rarely trust my first impressions, and I did right not to in this case. We turned off the main road past some municipal buildings and a petrol station, down a dusty road to the centre of town. I was going to be staying at the home of another volunteer called Anita. She had agreed to let me sleep in her spare room for a few days while I got myself sorted before finally heading out to Chinchimane. Anita was an old hand at VSO, having completed placements in Jamaica and Papua New Guinea in the 1960s and this, her second Namibian position, as she approached retirement. The volunteer network is strong, and I was amazed at how people went out of their way to assist us as we acclimatised. Anita was welcoming and wise and offered to show me around town.

The name Katima Mulilo means "quenches the fire" in the Silozi language and refers to the rapids of the nearby Zambezi River. A short walk from the town centre took us to the banks of the mighty river where hippos and crocs were resident. During the dry season elephants would wander to its banks to drink, and while I never spotted them that close to town, I did see their footprints and dung. I felt a surge of exhilaration and couldn't stop grinning; I was going to be living and working near one of the world's great rivers, evocative of so many adventures. There were various lodges dotted along the banks, but generally it was undeveloped.

We all met up for a drink that evening at the Zambezi River Lodge, the new volunteers and the five that had been living in Katima for the past year (three Brits and a

Dutch couple). I was the only one who would be living out of town, but it was a real comfort to know that this approachable, supportive group would be here.

After a good night's sleep, Anita pointed me in the right direction and armed with an umbrella for shade and a purse full of Namibian dollars I set off to explore. The town itself has a growing population of around 28,000 people mainly from the Masubia and Mafwe communities. Side roads were sandy with no pavements and although cars were infrequent, when they did pass, drivers were regularly compelled to put their foot down to avoid getting stuck in the soft sand. The main roads were potholed tarmac with sandy verges for pedestrians. The outskirts of town were residential. Anita's area was for middle-income families: avenues of single-story concrete houses with corrugated zinc roofs and neat gardens. More affluent properties were found nearer the river, and scruffy shanty towns of shacks developed off the main road out of town.

As with Windhoek, I was pleasantly surprised by the number and variety of shops in Katima. Those better read and better travelled than me may tut and shake their heads. What did I expect? Roadside piles of yams and bananas in a dustbowl? Ordinary, suburban life in

African countries is seldom portrayed in western media, so apologies for my initial lack of knowledge. There were South African chain stores such as PEP and Jet for clothes, Bears Furniture Store, a pharmacy, café, hardware shop and builders supply and an OK Superstore (which sold *Head & Shoulders,* tweezers and razors, thank God). I was surprised by the high number of Chinese stores. I did not realise how many Chinese people live throughout Africa. An estimated one million have moved to the continent over the past decade, and around 3–4,000 Chinese people are thought to live in Namibia. One of the government opposition parties puts the number as high as 40,000, arguing that Chinese construction workers are putting Namibians out of jobs. Most Namibians I spoke to were glad of Chinese immigration, as China is one of the few countries willing to offer investment and business opportunities rather than aid. Although some pointed out that money made flowed back to China rather than ending up in Nambian pockets.

I met up with Jane and Carol, two lovely English women who had been living in Katima for the past year. They gave me a tour of their favourite Chinese shops. They sold everything from food and toiletries to clothes, home furnishings and electrical items. I bought bedding, towels and some cooking utensils and crockery for my house.

Social events were organised including a grand lunch where all of the volunteers were introduced to the British High Commissioner to Namibia. I feel out of my depth in the company of very confident, privately educated people, (although less and less these days) and I didn't speak much. One of the volunteers had brought their young son along, at one point he shouted out "I can see someone with their elbows on the table", it was me.

The next day was spent on administrative duties. I needed to register with the Ministry of Education and open a bank account. I also needed to make a plan to actually head out to Chinchimane, see my house and school and meet my new colleagues, but I was in no rush to go. I enjoyed my time at Anita's house and hanging out with the other volunteers. I felt secure and looked after. The thought of heading out into the bush on my own was filling me with dread. Jane and Carol were attuned to my nervousness and asked if I would like them to come with me for a first visit. The plan was to go to the school to see my house and meet everyone, and then head back to Katima as we had a VSO education conference scheduled. I would go to the conference, then head to Chinchimane permanently in a week. They organised a lift the next day from a man called Joseph, who worked for the Ministry of Education. He pointed to the tattoo on my arm (one of those ubiquitous Celtic bands, acquired as a teenager in an attempt to look different) and asked whether I had been in prison. He said that in Namibia only street-fighting criminals had tattoos. I explained that I am about as far removed from a street-fighting criminal as it is possible to get. Joseph was kind and funny and pointed out landmarks so I could find my own way to the village next time. He told me he had spotted five elephants last time he had made this journey.

The road out to Chinchimane was a gravel road; the truck threw up clouds of dust as we rumbled along and if you opened the window, you got a face full of grit. The road had recently been graded so was in pretty good condition. Over the coming months, after the December rains, it became rutted and potholed, and the journey could take hours, depending on weather and conditions. In 2010, two years after I had returned to the UK, the road was tarmacked, and when I went back for a visit, we smoothly cruised to the village in forty-five minutes.

Away from the town, the concrete houses were replaced by traditional mud and thatch dwellings. In between small settlements the landscape was featureless, grey, dusty scrub with the occasional path running off amongst the camel thorn and acacia trees. Cattle and goats grazed on what little vegetation they could find, accompanied by herd boys – kids in tatty clothes brandishing sticks. This was the tail end of the dry season, and it hadn't rained for months; I didn't spot a single green shoot on the entire journey. Conversation in the truck dried up too. I didn't trust my voice to speak without an emotional crack. Could I really live out here? The holiday was over, and I was uneasy.

After about an hour of driving, Joseph took a left turn at a metal grain store and a blank metal sign. If you studied the sign up close you could make out the raised ghost of letters that spelt out Chinchimane, but the black paint had long since been sandblasted off. The gravel road petered out and became a sandy track. The truck skidded along past traditional mud and thatch houses, a church and a large, enclosed area that Joseph told me was the *khuta*, or traditional courthouse. Chinchimane is an important village in the region as it is home to Chief Mamili King of the Mafwe traditional authority. Joseph used the word tribe, but I am not sure that is a good translation. He said that I should visit the chief one day soon and pay my respects. I finally caught my first glimpse of Simataa Senior Secondary School, a concrete cluster of four long, low buildings painted cream and burgundy. The Namibian flag was flying in the courtyard, and a toothless old man in a blue boiler suit and cap was silently raking the sand. He looked up as we pulled in to park and gave us a wave.

Joseph escorted me straight to the principal's office, where Mrs Mahoto greeted me with a huge smile followed by a welcome, enveloping hug. She was a big, beautiful lady and as she hugged me, the enormous knot building in my stomach untied just a little bit. She told me they had been waiting for me for such a long time and that I was most welcome. The plan was to show me around my new home and the school, and then lessons would be suspended so that I could meet all the staff. A message was sent to gather the school board members (a collection of village elders with an equivalent role to our school governors) and the Chinchimane regional school inspector. Rather confusingly, both the head of the school board and the inspector were called Mr Mwilima.

Mrs Mahoto led the way across the schoolyard to the staff accommodation. She wanted to show me my new home before a tour of the school. When I first saw my house, I had to fight back tears because everyone was looking at me expectantly and smiling. It wasn't because the house was awful – far from it, it was much better than I had imagined it might be. The tears were because the enormity of what I was embarking on just hit me full in the stomach. I was overwhelmed by an instant, physical feeling of panic. I felt sick and scared, and I wanted to sob and go home. This was not a holiday in the sun surrounded by friends, drinking beers and exploring unknown places. This was me in a tiny village, miles from anywhere, with no running water, no electricity, no telephone and, right now, no friends. I managed a wobbly smile but had to keep quiet, not trusting my voice, and just nodding as Mrs Mahoto gave me a tour. It was a small, concrete, semi-detached, single-storey house with a metal roof and a shared, sandy yard. I had a kitchen, a loo and shower and a bigger room with a chair, desk, large cupboard and a bed in it. The floors were tiled, and the walls painted pale grey. It was sparse but spotlessly clean. Mrs Mahoto had clearly taken care to get the place looking good for my arrival. She turned on the kitchen tap, and clear water gushed out. "See," she said, "fresh water here." This was clearly some magical fluke; it was the one and only time that water flowed freely from the taps in my house for the next two years.

I was struggling to take everything in and unable to engage in pleasantries, so Jane and Carol filled the silence with chat, and Jane squeezed my hand as we headed over to the school. I gave her a watery smile and took a deep breath. As we walked through the school courtyard lessons stopped, and students lined the classroom windows waving at me and calling my name, "Susan, hello Susan, welcome to Simataa School." They were shushed and reprimanded by their teachers and were told, "It is Miss Ryding, not Susan to you." At home I am Sue; no one calls me Susan unless I am in big trouble and it sounded strange and foreign.

Mrs Mahoto beckoned two students to show me around. The head of science was currently away from school and the science laboratory was locked. So, a full tour would have to wait for another day. I was shown the five classrooms for grades 8 up to 12. The school had around a hundred and thirty students ranging in age from twelve to eighteen. As with other rural schools, most students were boarders, staying in the large hostel building 200m from the school site. The girls' hostel was secured behind an eight-foot wire fence to keep the girls in and the lads out. Dormitory rooms had four bunk beds in each, and the lack of posters and decoration of any sort struck me. The boys' hostel next door carried the whiff of teenage males: sweaty socks and emerging testosterone. We didn't linger. I tried to show interest and ask questions, but I was dazed and mostly remained silent. Months later, I learnt people had thought me quiet and a little standoffish on that first day as I had barely spoken. Jane said I looked terrified throughout the tour. I felt bad about that, as it certainly had not been my intended first impression. In truth, I had barely listened to what was going on around me and had instead been battling the urge to announce that I had made a big mistake and disappear off back home.

After the remainder of the tour, which took in the dining hall and vegetable garden, I was ushered into the staff room. The rest of the teachers were sitting around the edges of the room, and at one end, behind a table, was Mrs Mahoto and five men that, judging by their age, I assumed to be the school board members. I was introduced to Mr Mwilima, the school inspector, who was standing by the door. A single chair had been placed in the centre of the room and, to my horror, I was directed to sit in it. Everyone stared at me, and there were few smiles. Mrs Mahoto stood and made introductions. She gestured around the room presenting each of the staff members in turn. With so many new faces and unfamiliar sounding names, I had a battle to remember them. Mr Shamwazi (nice moustache) and Miss Siambango (huge smile) were the biology, geography and physical education teachers. They turned out to be two of the most brilliant teachers I know. Mr Dhlamini was from Zimbabwe and taught maths; he grinned at me. "At last, another foreigner to keep me company."

Mr Tatelo and Miss Simataa were Silozi language teachers. While all lessons in secondary school were delivered in English, Silozi was still studied at this level. Miss Mushe was the junior physical science teacher. She had only qualified that year and looked very young. I nodded and attempted a smile; I knew that working closely with Miss Mushe and helping her develop confidence in delivering practical science lessons was part of my remit. Miss Mutenda (gorgeous) was an English teacher along with Mr Chalo (enormous), and Mr Nzwala (very shiny head) was the deputy head teacher, referred to as the HoD. Due to lack of space, Miss Kambinda, the school secretary (beautiful) was perched on the knee of Miss Mayumbelo (great red dress), the life sciences teacher. If I'd had a crystal ball, I would have looked into the future and seen that these two women, Lynn and Josephine, were going to become two of the best friends I have ever had. I would see that in a few months' time, it would be me perched on Josephine's knee during staff meetings, trying not to laugh as she poked me in the ribs while Mrs Mahoto was talking, that I would carry Josephine's baby around in a papoose on my back and that I would make a speech when Lynn got married. But I didn't know this, and in that moment, I felt incredibly alone.

The announcements did not stop there. The second Mr Mwilima, head of the school board members, then stood and presented himself and his four colleagues. He was an astonishing-looking man, tall with thick, bushy hair (all of the other men had theirs shaved) and heavily pockmarked skin. I wondered whether he had suffered from smallpox as a boy. If so, he must have been one of the last people to get the disease. We became friends over the many months that I worked at the school, but I never had the courage to ask.

The final speaker was the other Mr Mwilima, the school inspector. He was a tall, handsome man who strode around the room, towering above me. He was confused about where I was from and declared that, "Miss Ryding, Susan, has arrived from America to help us at this school. She is going to share her ideas and help us to improve. In America they have this great thing called the working lunch, and I hope very much that Susan is going to introduce us to the working lunch. No more sitting idle in the middle of the day but working harder, harder, harder all of the time." Oh, dear God, everyone was going to hate me.

My house in Chinchimane

Simataa Senior Secondary School

CHAPTER 2

MR SIMATAA

Simataa is a common name in parts of Namibia. It is used as a first name or a surname. Mr Malapo told me that it was a Lozi name that meant "bad-tempered". In one grade 9 class of forty-three learners, there were twelve Simataas, including one Simataa Simataa. Simataa Simataa from Simataa School. Mr Alfred Simataa was the head of science at Simataa Senior Secondary School and, as such, would be my close colleague.

Mr Simataa was away on a course when I first arrived, and as time went on, I realised that he went away on courses a lot. I kept a tally of the days Mr Simataa spent out of class on courses, and the count had reached seventy-three by the end of my twenty-seven-month post. These were not courses specifically related to teaching but concerned with his private study, working towards a degree through NAMCOL (Namibian College of Open Learning) distance learning. Supply teachers did not exist, and although he was instructed to leave cover work for his classes, he rarely did. With one textbook between six, his students struggled to keep up with their work when he was away. Mr Simataa greeted me enthusiastically when we first met, believing I would step in to teach his classes any time he felt he had more pressing matters to attend to. His understanding of my role and the principal's expectations of me were quite different.

As head of science, Mr Simataa was responsible for the laboratory, which I was desperate to see. Unfortunately, there was only one key, and he kept it, so I had to wait a few days until he returned. I asked the other teachers and some of the learners how frequently they used the school laboratory. The short answer was "never". Occasionally, grade 12 students had classes in there, but never practical lessons. Other science teachers were not allowed to use equipment without Mr Simataa's permission, which he rarely gave. This did not seem to be through meanness but rather a desire to protect the equipment and resources, there being very little budget to replace items.

I understood his desire to keep everything intact, but if it was never used, we could not show that a working lab was essential to effective science lessons. Mrs Mahoto asked me to take over responsibility for the laboratory and start introducing weekly practical lessons. In particular, she wanted me to work with Miss Precious Mushe, who was in her first year of teaching and lacked confidence in some of the topics. I asked Precious whether she had ever used the laboratory, the answer was again "no". Mrs Mahoto said that we needed to make proper use of the laboratory, monitor its impact on student attainment and then build a case that would allow her to request adequate funds to maintain it properly. We could not demonstrate the positive influence of practical work in science learning if no one had access to the laboratory.

It would be useful at this point to explain how the education system worked in the Zambezi Region and the role that VSO played in its development. During the apartheid era, which ran from 1948 until the early 1990s, Black Namibians did not receive the same education opportunities as white children. Government spending was approximately a tenth for them as for their white counterparts, and few Black teachers were university educated. Black learners were taught agriculture instead of physical science and further maths. After independence, things changed rapidly, but there was a deficit of expertise. Qualified science teachers who had not been taught the subject themselves and had little or no practical experience were coming through the ranks. Part of Namibia's Vision 2030 is to promote science and educate engineers and doctors in the country. Vision 2030 is a political framework that outlines the fundamental transformation of the Namibian political and economic landscape. It is an optimistic document that sets out a hopeful vision for Namibia's future – it is only three pages long and worth reading. This is where VSO came in. Volunteer teacher trainers and advisory teachers were recruited in maths and physical science. Due to unrest in the Zambezi Region and the failed uprising of 1999 in which fourteen people were killed, it was deemed unsafe for volunteers until 2004.

In September 2004, a Dutch science teacher called Kees arrived along with his wife to take up the post as a physical science advisory teacher. He was an experienced head of science who had already completed a VSO position in Botswana. He set up a laboratory at the Teacher's Resource Centre in Katima Mulilo, successfully applied for a large grant from the Petro Chemical Fund and began stocking the laboratory with equipment and chemicals which could be distributed to schools. He ran workshops where teachers could practise using equipment and wrote a scheme of work incorporating demonstrations and class practicals. In 2005, Carol and Jane joined him as physical science teacher trainers. They were based in Katima Combined School and Caprivi Secondary School. Their role involved supporting teachers within their school and the wider region through team teaching, production of teaching resources and development of the school laboratories. I was to perform a similar role at Simataa Senior Secondary School. The difference was I was based in a rural school, 60km from Katima.

The region was divided into eight different education circuits. I worked in the Chinchimane Circuit, which contained three senior secondary schools (up to grade 12) and six primary schools. A school inspector, Mr Mwilima, was assigned to the circuit office in Chinchimane village and it was his job to monitor and support the schools in his circuit. Workshops and training events could be held in the circuit office, and resources should be shared between schools. This was a wonderful idea in theory, but in practice the schools were too far apart and transport too unreliable to allow any meaningful movement of people, equipment or ideas. It was difficult to communicate messages to the remote village schools as mobile phone networks did not cover these regions at that time.

Kees decided to shelve the circuit model and instead held all training events and equipment libraries in the Teacher's Resource Centre in town. All the teachers travelled to town at least once a month, and often once a week. Hitching a lift, or "hiking" as it was called, was much easier when travelling from one of the villages into town, particularly on a Friday. Initially, the focus was on grade 11 and 12 (broadly comparable to GCSE and AS classes in England and Wales); after two years this was extended to include grade 10. At this stage, it was felt that with our limited resources and time, attempting to work with primary schools as well would be too difficult. VSO's priorities have since changed and it is good to see early years learning taking priority these days. I was lucky that someone as experienced as Kees preceded my placement. It meant that there was a strategy in place and a practised leader behind it. I love being in the classroom and was keen to balance my training role with classroom teaching. I needed to see the reality of teaching large, poorly resourced classes if I was to develop a sustainable plan. Mrs Mahoto was incredibly supportive and allowed me to produce my own timetable, ensuring I got wide teaching experience alongside plenty of non-contact time to carry out other work.

Of course, my non-teaching time would only be of value if I could actually get into the laboratory and get cracking. Three days after my arrival, Mr Simataa returned with the key and I finally got to have a look around. He was very apologetic as we entered. "Our facilities are very poor. We are lacking in equipment and chemicals. We cannot use this laboratory for any meaningful work." He told me repeatedly that I needed to secure funding to build a new, fully equipped lab. He assumed that I would be able to access substantial pots of money and was disappointed when I explained that the only resource on offer was me. I already had insecurities about whether I was good enough to do this job, and his comments did not help my confidence. The room was dusty and cluttered. Small wooden desks and chairs covered the floor space. The row of dirty sinks under one window were full of insect corpses, some of which looked interesting. In between the teacher's desk and the blackboard was a door leading to a small chemical store and prep room. Boxes and crates were stacked precariously around the edges of the room. I opened a few boxes and found they were packed with glassware: test tubes, beakers, conical flasks and measuring cylinders. Under the sinks were rows of microscopes; cardboard boxes of unused circuit boards complete with wires, cells and bulbs were heaped higgledy-piggledy on top of one another. The chemical store was sparse, and much of what was there looked old and corroded, but I knew that I could restock this easily from Kees's resource centre in town. I told Mr Simataa that the lab was much better equipped than I was expecting. He tutted, "No, no, we need more resources." I told him I would like to stay in the lab and start making an inventory and work out what was lacking. Perhaps he could leave the key with me, and I would lock up when I had finished. He said I could return it in the morning.

I had wondered why Mrs Mahoto didn't insist on making more copies of the lab key. The next morning at first light, I hitchhiked into town to do just that. Staff at the hardware shop informed me that there were no facilities for key cutting in Katima; I would need to travel to

Rundu, 500km away, or cross the border into Botswana. I hadn't thought to bring my passport. Keys were coded, and the store kept multiple copies of each code (which I thought rendered the idea of a secure lock rather redundant) but did not stock this particular key. The only answer was to fit a new lock. I had no experience of fitting locks but assumed it would be doubly difficult with no power tools. With no easy access to the laboratory, my work would be impossible. I bought a new lock, then walked to the Ministry of Works to register a job card: "new lock fitted on school laboratory door, estimated time for completion: three weeks." On my return to school that evening, I explained my plan to Mr S. He said it was a good idea and that we needed to get the laboratory organised properly so that people could see how poor it was and build us a new one.

I liked Mr Simataa; he was funny and intelligent, but I found him difficult to work with. We had different ideas about education and about what the focus of my job should be. He was a short man of around fifty years old; he wore his hair quite long and had large, thick glasses. The glasses continually slipped down his nose, and he was forever pushing them back up again. Students hone in on any repetitive physical or verbal tic and use it to their advantage. They performed great impressions of him, although their gentle mocking seemed affectionate to me. Mr Simataa was deeply religious and a member of the Church of the Seventh-day Adventists. I was ignorant of his religion and researched the beliefs of the SDA. They are the twelfth-largest religious body in the world, with a strong missionary presence around the globe. Seventh-day Adventists believe in the infallibility of Scripture and adhere to the Ten Commandments. The Sabbath day is a Saturday, running from Friday evening to Saturday evening. Followers traditionally lead a socially conservative life, eschewing rock music, alcohol and even rejecting jewellery and theatre as being too frivolous. Soon after we met, Mr Simataa told me an amazing story about how he had encountered God twice in visions and had once been lifted to Heaven by God's right hand. We were drinking tea in my house, and he began his tale; it was well-rehearsed, and it was clear he enjoyed having a fresh audience. I had never seen him so animated. He rapturously described the golden and dazzling lights of Heaven, so bright and blinding that they had permanently damaged his sight, hence the enormous glasses. Mr Simataa (I never once called him Alfred) had been an intellectual exile in Britain during the Namibian fight for independence and lived in Selly Oak in Birmingham for six years. I was a student at Birmingham University and lived in Selly Oak for three years; it turned out that in 1996 we were living on parallel streets. Small world. It felt serendipitous, and although our relationship was a difficult one, I grew fond of him, and there was much to enjoy in his company.

Mr Simataa had many brilliant stories. A couple he lodged with in Birmingham gave him an upright piano. He had learnt how to play and on his return to an independent Namibia had posted the piano home. He visited the Post Office in Katima Mulilo every Friday for one and a half years before it finally arrived. Sadly, the journey and subsequent heat had rendered it horribly out of tune, and without a piano tuner, it now sat useless in his home. It must have been difficult for him to have a foreign woman half his age arrive and start making demands. How would I feel now if a twenty-something teacher from the Philippines or Finland (their education systems consistently top the Programme for International Student Assessment ranking) arrived at my UK school and started telling me how to improve? I know exactly how I would feel. I would resent them. I tried, to begin with at least, to take on tasks that he asked me to do. I started on the equipment inventory, restocked the chemical cupboard, and taught some revision classes. However, I knew I needed to do more, and Mrs Mahoto was insistent that I should take control of the lab and ensure that all science teachers and all learners had regular access to it. It became clear that it would be impossible to accomplish this without treading on his toes.

The Namibian academic year runs from January to December, and I had arrived at the tail end of one. I asked Mrs Mahoto if I could be involved in writing the timetable for next year, and so ensure that all science classes had at least one double practical lesson a week in the laboratory. She said it would be best if I just wrote the whole timetable. The school was small, but this was still quite a daunting task, confounded by the bizarre seven-day cycle it observed. It started logically. Monday was day one, running through to day five on Friday. However, the following Monday became day six and Tuesday day seven, only returning to day one by Wednesday. I think it was a throwback to boarding school education where they had "prep" at the weekends. The most frequently asked question in the staff room was,

"What day is it?"

"Tuesday."

"No, what number day is it?"

"Oh, two, no, maybe three."

To complicate things even more, if there were no lessons for a day – it could be a national holiday or school had to be closed due to lack of water – on our return we would go back to the day we had missed. For example, let's say it's Wednesday, and it's day four on the timetable and on Thursday school is closed for Independence Day. When we returned to school on Friday, it would be classed as day five. I feel muddled just writing about it.

I had visited Chinchimane Primary School and Kanono Junior School recently to plan a regular visit to do some team teaching and science club activities. They both worked to sensible five-day timetables, and if school was closed on a Thursday, it was still Friday when you went back. This made it practically impossible for me to align my free periods with their timetable. I explained this problem to Mrs Mahoto and Mr Nzwala. After lengthy discussions, they agreed we could use a five-day system, but this would still be numerical, and if we missed a day, that day must still be maintained on return. Their logic was that we would end up missing too many days otherwise. I tried to point out that the actual number of teaching days remained the same, but they were immovable. I was grateful for the changes they'd agreed to and didn't want to push my luck. Eventually, I produced a timetable in which every physical science class had one double period a week in the laboratory, and biology, life science and agriculture had opportunities to book the room when needed. Mr Simataa seemed pleased but pointed out that we would need bigger tables and more chairs: that was next on my list.

After I had been at the school for about a month, Mr Simataa asked me whether I would like to attend church with him one Saturday. I am not a religious person, but I was raised a Catholic and I feel at home in places of worship. Churches hold memories from the happiest and saddest milestones in people's lives. I do not believe in God, and a formal service is not for me, but I do enjoy spending time in churches, absorbing their peace and sense of history. Missionaries have marched across the continent and eroded traditions and culture, making people feel ashamed of what they believe in. That aside, I was interested in visiting Mr Simataa's church and wondered whether we might bond over the experience. Some learners came to collect me early on Saturday morning. They gave me a piece of material called a *shetenga* and said that I must wear it to show respect. I put in on my head, *hijab* style, and they burst out laughing. "No, no Susan, you wear it like this," they giggled, tying it around their waist. Respectfully dressed, we set off walking through the sand. I could hear the wonderful choir already and reasoned that even if the sermon meant little to me, I could enjoy some amazing music.

Mr Simataa was already there when I arrived, busy up at the front preparing to deliver some of the service. He indicated that I should sit with the learners. Mine was the only white face, and people kept turning around and grinning at me. Quite a few came to greet me and shake me by the hand, which was lovely. Some small children burst into tears, which was less enjoyable. One stooped old woman, wearing a brilliant top with fishnet sleeves that had "HOT Jennifer Lopez" sequinned across the chest, gripped my hand and tried to lead me to the front. I couldn't understand what she was saying, so the girls translated between fits of giggles. "She wants you to come up and to sing an English hymn for us." A weedy rendition of *Away in a Manger* would do none of us any good, so I feigned non-comprehension and, eventually, she gave up. The service was extremely long, and every time I thought it might be ending, we simply got up and moved into groups for Bible study, then back into church for more lectures. An earnest young man in a smart, shiny suit took it upon himself to translate everything into English for me, delivering his whispered interpretations closely and rather sweatily into my ear. At one point, a pastor started ranting in English about how evolution wasn't true. I just kept my head down and tried to look holy. Four hours in, I wished I had eaten more for breakfast.

When the service finally ended, I invited Mr Simataa round for some hot chocolate. He had mentioned how much he loved hot chocolate and a friend had posted some sachets of Cadbury's Options the week before. He told me about his wife and daughter, currently in Zambia but due to return after Christmas. This surprised me, I had assumed he was single, married to the church. His wife was Zambian and was struggling to get work in Katima despite being a qualified accountant. Namibian law dictates that if there is a Namibian national capable of doing a job, they should be given that post even if

48

there are immigrants better qualified or more experienced to do it. The Namibians I met could be derogatory toward their Zambian neighbours across the Zambezi, frequently accusing them of paddling over illegally in *macoros*[2] and stealing things. Mr Simataa's wife, Rachel, had spent most of their married life back home with her family but would be moving over permanently in January. His daughter, Claire, was four, and he was clearly proud of her. I asked Lynn about Rachel, and she said that she was beautiful and clever, and she didn't really know why such a woman had married such a man. Perhaps he had used one of Mr Tatelo's love potions?

Some weeks later, when Rachel and Claire finally arrived, I invited the family over for a meal. I cooked spaghetti bolognese, which Claire thought was brilliant, "like small snakes". Rachel was lovely, and that night was the beginning of a friendship that still lasts today. She would borrow books – Agatha Christie was a particular favourite – and Claire would do some drawing and shyly ask to try on some of my necklaces and bracelets. Over time, we talked about Mr Simataa and

---

[2] A *macoro* is a wooden canoe, roughly carved from a single tree trunk.

how, as frustrating as he was to work with, he was even more frustrating to live with. Rachel told me he gave her very little money to buy food or electricity for their home in town and that she frequently had to go without meals. A teacher earns a decent enough salary in Namibia, and I was not aware that Mr Simataa had any other dependants.

I did not understand how he could do this, and I lost some respect for him. However, the bottom line was he was my colleague and, if I were to have any impact during my time here, we needed to work harmoniously together.

I worked hard to get the lab ready for the new academic year, when I hoped it would be in regular use. Mrs Mahoto allocated some of the school budget for new furniture, and I had some money that friends from home had donated. I visited the government stores and picked out large tables and two big, metal cupboards for storing equipment. I bought paint and material to make curtains. A group of grade 12 learners scrubbed and painted while singing along to my wind-up radio, which they thought was hilarious. The worth of a radio seemed to hinge on how many batteries it took. "See, Miss Ryding, mine is good, it takes eight big ones. Yours takes none, it is very poor."

I made lined curtains to block out light if necessary, which would be useful for some of the physics lightbox experiments. Miss Mushe moved some old boxes out and stacked equipment in the new cupboards, which could be locked for security. The UN had donated wooden boxes of life science kit some years before, and many of these lay unused against the walls. When I dragged one away, I found that the entire back had been eaten by termites. Conical flasks and glass funnels had been incorporated into the walls of their mound, like windows. It reminded me of the plaster of Paris ant nests I had made as a child in primary school. We painted a huge periodic table on the back wall, and I put up some posters. In time, I planned to decorate the walls with examples of outstanding work produced by the students. I cleared out the chemical store cupboard and made a note of what needed replacing. Anything that looked discoloured or corroded was put in a box to be taken to the Teacher's Resource Centre for safe disposal (I'm pretty sure that this meant being buried in a deep hole). Mr Simataa, Miss Mushe and I made a list of laboratory rules, which I printed, laminated and stuck to the door. I was really pleased with the finished room: all it needed to be a success was students.

The Seventh-day Adventist church in Chinchimane

Mr Simataa

CHAPTER 3
THE TATELOS

As I was looking around my new home for the first time, there was a shout of "co co" (knock knock) and a beautiful, tall lady in her thirties and a small, grubby girl appeared in the doorway. This was my neighbour, Florence Tatelo, and her youngest child, Mumbiya. Mumbiya was three years old, snotty, scowling and drinking cold tea from a plastic bottle. Florence, two kids and her husband (Mr Tatelo, a Silozi language teacher at the school) lived next door in a house the same size as mine. Florence squeezed my hand and told me she was really pleased to have me as a new neighbour; Mumbiya chattered away and offered me a swig of her tea. Florence admitted months later that she and Mr Tatelo had been very nervous about having an English woman move in next door. The only other white people they had met were some folks in town who still referred to themselves as South West Africans (South West Africa was the name given to Namibia under the apartheid regime) and they had been worried that we would not get on. Florence was an impressive woman, and I respected and admired her more and more as I got to know her. She had been married before, but her husband had died, leaving her to raise two children on her own. She had met and married Mr Tatelo, and they had had two more children together. The older ones, Emily and Likando, now boarded at our school, while Mumbiya and her six-year-old brother, Mukena, lived at home.

Florence was a devout Christian and fulfilled a significant traditional role in the family: cooking, cleaning, fetching water, tending the crops, pounding maize and taking care of the children. She also ran a number of diverse businesses on the side: selling mobile phone top-ups and home-grown vegetables and crocheting tablecloths and handkerchiefs. As a welcome gift, Florence gave me a collection of crocheted antimacassars and luminous yellow doilies, for which I've never quite found the right place. She also made "fat cakes" to sell to the teachers and learners at break time.

Fat cakes (or "fat cooks", or simply "fats") were absolutely delicious, and I was on three a day for a while. They were small doughnuts deep-fried in oil, and Florence would make them fresh each day on an open fire. It cost 10 cents for three, wrapped in a twist of newspaper.

The break time ritual became my favourite time of day; it was a million miles away from the stressed, fractious staff room break in England. I would wander across the yard from school and put the kettle on or collect some hot water from Florence's pot on the fire if the gas was empty. Filter coffee cost a fortune; it was my luxury item as the instant Camp coffee was cut with hickory and tasted grim. I strained it through a clean sock as a cafetiere seemed a luxury too far. I would then sit by Florence's fire where she crouched over a sizzling pan of delicious fats. I rolled mine in sugar and occasionally injected them with runny jam using the syringe from my VSO-issued first aid kit. Mumbiya would come and sit on my knee and chatter away in Silozi, rubbing snot on my work clothes and telling me about her morning. I taught her to say "mmmm, delicious" and rub her tummy before we started eating, which made everyone laugh.

In those first overwhelming months, Florence really looked after me and stopped me from making a number of social blunders. When I hung my knickers on our shared washing line, she discreetly brought them inside. "People should not see these, Susan, they will be queueing from the tar road for a closer look." When I asked her whether it would be appropriate for me to visit the small bars or shebeens in the village and buy a beer, she told me, "No, the only women who go there are prostitutes."

We would sit in the shade of our front porch in the afternoon, and she would ask me about life in England and tell me about life in the village. She encouraged me to take an afternoon nap, saying it was good for my health. Florence would often drag her mattress outside for a snooze in the midday heat. She told me that I should sleep indoors though, as I was too pale to sleep outside, and the mosquitoes would eat me. Alongside all her other endeavours, Florence was studying to pass her physical science iGCSE and asked me whether I would help with some of her assignments. She hadn't studied the subject at school, and her distance learning course was tough, with little face to face support. I told her she should come along to some of the lessons I taught, but she said that would be frowned on by the learners and other teachers; they wouldn't want a stupid old woman in their class. I didn't believe this, but to avoid a fuss I agreed to meet up with her some evenings and weekends for tuition.

Those evenings were some of my favourite times. We would wait for the hum of the diesel generator, then head over to the laboratory. I would help Florence go through some questions and practise calculations. Her knowledge was weak, but we had fun. Sometimes we would go through an experiment described in the textbook, and this was where her strengths lay. She was practically minded and became an expert at electrical circuits, which was a rather redundant skill in our village.

One evening, on our way home in the dark, I was about to step off the concrete pavement onto the sand when Florence grabbed me and pulled me back. We heard a hiss, and when I looked down there was a cobra coiled right where my foot would land. It may be stretching it a little to say that Florence saved my life that night, but that's the story we liked to tell.

Florence taught me about local cuisine and cooked several Caprivian specialties, but the fat cakes remained my favourite. Namibian food is generally fairly bland and carbohydrate heavy. It doesn't involve the aromatic spices and herbs associated with some other African dishes. Heavily influenced by South Africa and very meat orientated, favourite dishes are pap, chicken, goat or beef, *chakalaka* (vegetable and tomato relish), *sosaties* (skewered meat) and fresh or dried fish. Being so close to the Zambezi River, there was a plentiful supply of barbel fish (catfish), tigerfish, and Zambezi bream at the market. The fresh fish was gorgeous, but I found the dried too strong in flavour and difficult to stomach. Sometimes Florence cooked it in a stew, and she always made a watered-down version for me. Pap is ground maize meal cooked with water to make a thick porridge. It is a staple across much of Africa and comes under many names: *ugali* in Tanzania, *nshima* in Zambia and mealy meal in South Africa, to name but a few. I really liked pap, although mine was always a bit watery when I cooked it myself. Josephine said I was too weak to stir it properly. I taught her the word "wimp", which she took great delight in calling me. It was real comfort food: filling but nutritionally quite poor. Whenever I cooked pasta or potatoes for Josephine, she would complain that she wasn't satisfied with the meal and go home for some pap. Florence was very thoughtful and would often pop over with something for me to try – a fresh papaya from her tree, some greens from the garden or some soup she had made. She had an uncanny knack for knowing when I was feeling homesick or lonely, and appeared bearing gifts at some of my lowest moments. Once when I was ill, she brought around a meal with a note that said, "may the Lord God be the doctor and the caretaker during this tough time. May you be healed by the soft touch of our Lord." It was just about the best tonic.

The most common meat eaten was chicken, and although numerous hens strolled around the village, most teachers at school seemed to buy theirs frozen from the supermarket. Astonishingly, this was imported from South America. Beef was also popular, and this was frequently sold by the roadside where a slaughtered animal would be hung from a tree and portions hacked off when required, in a buzzing haze of flies. I was nervous about buying meat this way, but I accompanied Lynn and Josephine a couple of times. Butchery skills appeared absent, and rather than request specific cuts the ladies ordered unappealing sounding "lumps" by gesturing at specific areas. Florence would often come back from the village with a bucket of meat and tripe that would sit outside the back door. Goats were common in the village too, although I rarely came across them to eat and goat meat wasn't for sale in the supermarket. Lynn said most people kept and slaughtered their own goats rather than buying and selling them. Meat was not usually left to hang before being eaten, and as a result it was pretty tough. This issue was overcome by simmering it for hours, often over a fire in a cute round pot called a *poitje*. Sometimes Florence would peg strips of beef on our shared washing line to cure in the sun. I always gave it a quick wipe before I hung out my clothes to be on the safe side.

Many families relied on their own crops for food staples, leaving them vulnerable in times of drought. Large villages had communal grain stores where food was stockpiled for lean times. Florence and Mr Tatelo's millet crop had ripened, the *mahangu* heads had dried, and now it was time to pound it into flour. A few miles past Kanono was a village called Lizao, and here was a mill where people could pay for sacks of corn to be ground. It cost N$25 to mill a sack of maize, and Mr

Tatelo said that this was too expensive, so in their household the job was left to Florence.

A hollowed-out *mopane* trunk was used as a large pestle and a second piece of wood, shaped as a sturdy, rounded pole about 2.5 metres long, acted as a mortar. Florence would place dried kernels into the base and raise the pole high, pounding down repeatedly to crush the grains and release the white powder. Once ground, it was sieved to remove any husk and then it was placed in sacks ready to be used. It was incredibly labour-intensive, and I could hear the thump, thump of pounding throughout the afternoon. I went over to Florence's yard with Lynn and Josephine to see if we could help. Joso and Lynn had the technique mastered as they used to help their mothers pound the maize when they were kids. They lifted the heavy pole up above their shoulders, dropping it into the wooden base then catching it on the upward bounce ready for the next drive, but they were rusty and their arms soon tired. I was hopeless as usual and felt my muscles burning and the palms of my hands rubbed raw within minutes. Florence was a machine and sang as she lifted and dropped the heavy pole time after time. I suspected that if Mr T was responsible for the pounding, he would have been able to find the cash for the mill.

The Tatelos and I shared a yard, so a few months after arriving, when I decided that I would like to get a dog, I had to ask their permission. Jane and Carol had adopted three scruffy dogs; one had been hit by a car and kept weeing on her bandaged leg. We called her "Smells Of Pissy Dog", although her real name was Star. Another was psychotic and chased and often bit passers-by; he was called Fox and, while a liability, he was also a super guard dog. The third was Speedo, who turned out to be pregnant. She gave birth to four pups, and I agreed to take one back to the village. He was yellow and looked a bit Labradorish, and I named him Jude. The Tatelos were happy for Jude to share their yard and agreed to look after him any weekends I went away, and finally adopted him when I went back home. A guard dog was quite a status symbol, and Mr Tatelo was under the misapprehension that Jude was a pedigree dog. I explained that the reason he looked so good was not down to breeding, but because I fed him and kept him flea and tick free.

Everyone was pretty horrified when I allowed him into the house; Josephine said it was like having a cow in there – smelly and dirty. I made him a small bed out of a cardboard box and fed him milk, pap and a few bits of meat. He was tiny and cried the first night, but soon settled in. He kept shaking his head and trying to scratch his ears, so I looked inside. Three engorged ticks were nestled inside each ear canal. With gritted teeth, I carefully twisted them out with my tweezers and then bathed the inside of his ears with Body Shop lavender and tea tree oil. Josephine said that he was better cared for than any of her children. Jude proceeded to eat the removed ticks, which, while pretty gross, turned out to be the least of his unappealing habits.

He started following me everywhere and frequently came to school. He would sit quietly at the front of the class for a while, but then he'd get bored and wreak havoc, nipping the students, stealing chalk and widdling on the floor. At this point, I would send him home to Florence, and she would tie him up. Eventually, he became too fat to wriggle under the yard gate and so was easier to control, until he got big enough to leap over it. He followed me when I went out on my bike and once trotted halfway to Kanono. At this point, he became exhausted and collapsed in a heap under a tree. He waited for three hours and then followed me back home. I had never owned a dog before, so wasn't sure of the best way to train one. He definitely needed some discipline as he was becoming delinquent. He frequently jumped up, once dramatically ripping my flimsy summer dress and exposing my (thankfully substantial) knickers to a hysterical group of pupils. I devoted some time to training sessions, backed up by Mr Tatelo, who would whack him if he got too feisty. The most mortifying aspect of Jude's behaviour was that he frequently got an erection whenever he saw me and would try to vigorously hump me if I was sitting down. Lynn and Josephine started referring to him as the boyfriend and latterly, as the amorous behaviour showed no sign of stopping, the husband. I resorted to the Mr Tatelo training method of a swift whack or boot, and this eventually seemed to do the trick.

Jude was the top dog in Chinchimane as he was well fed and strong. Many dogs in Namibia have a pretty hard time and packs of feral dogs roamed around, causing trouble. With no permanent vet in town, neutering was rarely carried out. They were periodically rounded up and shot if numbers got too high or there was an outbreak of rabies or anthrax. It was fairly common to see horrifically injured dogs slowly dying at the roadside. I saw one caught in a wire fence, bleeding and screaming, and wanted to try to free it. Mr Tatelo said it was too dangerous as it would bite and may be diseased. I asked whether he would shoot it, but he said he was out of ammunition. We left it there and the next day, when I went to check, it was dead. Life could be grim for animals in Chinchimane, and this was difficult to witness. I felt incapable of doing anything about it and developed a protective indifference that thankfully did not remain on my return home.

During a lesson one day, a howling dog ran back and forth past the laboratory window. It kept reaching round, crazily trying to bite something on its own back, probably driven manic by fleas or ticks. The students thought it hilarious; the image of the wretched thing has stayed with me for years. Despite a nationally ambivalent attitude towards dogs, the Tatelos took great care of Jude and two years later, when they bought a house in town, Jude went to live there as a guard dog. By that time, I was leaving in a couple of months anyway, but I did miss him. Shortly afterwards, he suffered a horrible injury, a perfectly circular, deep hole underneath his shoulder. It was the circumference of a penny and looked to be about 5cm deep, as if he had been impaled on a spike. It wasn't healing and we were worried that it might get infected. There was no vet in

Katima so I asked the handsome pharmacist for some advice. He sold me an extortionately-priced bottle of bright purple antiseptic spray and I passed on the instructions to Florence. When I dropped by to check on him a week later, he had been sprayed completely purple and the wound was healing nicely. Jude lived a long and happy life with the Tatelos; he remembered me when I visited a few years later. Florence phoned me when he died at the grand old age of ten and we shed a tear together.

Water was a problem in Chinchimane. A pipeline ran from Katima along the roadside to the villages, carrying treated, drinkable Zambezi water. The problematic issue was water pressure. By the time the pipeline reached Chinchimane, the pressure was too low for water to make it to individual houses. There were two communal taps in the village and one in the school grounds. Water generally made it to these, although on occasion they too ran dry. The daily routine was to collect containers of water from the school tap, usually done by the women or girls, and carry them home, balanced on the head. Florence tried to teach me how to carry a five-litre water container on my head, much to the students' amusement, but I was pretty hopeless. Few female teachers could manage it either; it was a dying skill amongst the educated, professional classes. The largest item I ever saw transported on the head was a wooden wardrobe, the smallest (and my favourite), a solitary tin of peas. Florence advised me that during the evening and through the night water pressure increased as fewer people were switching their taps on. During these hours there would be a steady drip from ours. She instructed me to wedge dishes and pans under every tap (there were only two, one in the kitchen and one in the washroom), and by morning there would be enough for a wash and a cup of tea.

I found it hard work to wash my long hair properly with such scant water, so I asked Josephine to cut it for me. We attempted a chic bob; there was something of the Amazonian tribesman about my fringe, but it was a pretty good job considering she had never cut hair before. She said I should burn the cut hair as people from the village would steal it to make love potions. Apparently, *makuwa* (white person) hair is worth a fortune to witch doctors. I ignored her advice and dropped it in my rubbish pit. The next day it had all gone, and there had been lots of it. Blown away maybe, although the pit was deep and other paper rubbish remained. Perhaps taken by weaver birds to thread into their nest. I asked Florence what she thought, and she laughed and said definitely stolen for magic.

 Occasionally, and usually after heavy rain, water would gush from the taps with substantial force. I was caught out a couple of times, resulting in small floods. Another trick was to collect rainwater in basins for washing clothes, although this was only possible for a small window every year. The Zambezi rainy season runs from late November until early March, with December being the wettest month. When I moved there in September, it hadn't rained for over six months and the town was a dust bowl. It didn't rain until November, and when it finally started it was a real event. The scent of rain on dry earth came number thirty-five in a recent poll of Britain's top fifty smells, beaten by fish and chips, bacon cooking and roast dinners. We Brits are a predictable bunch. It even has its own name: petrichor, derived from the Greek *petros* meaning stone and *ichor* the name given to the fluid flowing through the veins of mythological gods. I love that smell at home where it rains practically every day, so imagine the intensity of the scent when the ground has been dry for months. It was overwhelming, and I would stand and breathe it in like an expensive perfume.

The raindrops were fat, and I really wanted to run outside and dance. I settled for sitting on the porch with Florence and watching the kids dash about madly, laughing and screaming. Within hours huge millipedes and beetles had emerged from dormancy, and in a few days the sand was spiked with green, and the camel thorn tree in my garden was producing buds. It rained most days for a few months, usually at around four in the afternoon. Sometimes in the early evening there would be a dramatic thunderstorm with forked and sheet lightning, the likes of which I had never seen. One night, with a storm raging directly overhead, I was terrified that the tree overhanging our house would be hit. I dashed next door to ask the Tatelos if they were worried and whether we should evacuate. Mr Tatelo said God would protect us and suggested I go back to sleep.

One day, Mr Tatelo decided we should all venture out on a day trip to Lianshulu Lodge. Everyone contributed something towards a shared lunch, and we each gave Mr Tatelo N$10 for fuel. We set off on Sunday morning, six of us in the back and Florence and the children up front. Lianshulu Lodge is one of the oldest and most luxurious lodges in Namibia; at the time it cost N$3,500 for a room (which is what I earned in a month), and many guests arrived by private charter flight on the lodge's airstrip. It was absolutely gorgeous, tucked away on the banks of the Kwando River – a magnificent safari retreat.

Mr Tatelo drove right up to the front entrance, radio blaring and with a little shower of gravel as he skidded to a halt. An immaculately dressed man appeared instantly; he looked a little shocked to see our ramshackle crew but was very polite and asked, deadpan, whether we had a reservation. Mr Tatelo got out of the truck and announced that he was bringing an important visitor from Britain (pronounced Britane) who wished to have a look around. He gestured to me in the back. I blushed. He said my parents would be visiting soon, and I wanted to see whether this lodge was of a suitable standard to house them. The man smiled and said that the lodge was currently empty, with all of the guests out on safari and new ones only arriving late that evening, so he would show us around himself. He was lovely and clearly realised that none of us had the money to stay there. He took time to show us one of the suites and the gorgeous bar and veranda area. He said that the guests would be returning soon, and we were welcome to stay for our picnic, but would we mind eating it in the staff area?

One of Mr Tatelo's nephews worked there as a handyman, and he was called for and led us around the back. It reminded me of the scene where Baby carries the watermelon round to the staff digs behind the Kellerman's holiday chalets. The lodge was pristine and impressive, but the staff quarters were gloriously lively, and music thumped as kids played, people chatted, and food was cooked on open fires. A handsome safari guide with long dreadlocks roared up on a motorbike and came to say hello. He flirted outrageously, and Mr Tatelo and Florence got cross and sent him away. "He is not a good man, Susan, he is a gangster, and he will not be good." My fleeting dream of whizzing around Namibia on the back of his motorbike was dashed.

On the drive home, we stopped at the Tatelo's family village so I could see their home. The Chinchimane house was just for work, and they travelled home most weekends. It was a beautiful traditional mud house with a thatched roof. Nearby was their farmland, where the maize would soon be planted. It was close to the river, and Mr Tatelo said that they really suffered as hippos frequently came and grazed his crops. He had been given a special licence to shoot one particularly aggressive male, but it was a dangerous job, and he was worried about getting injured. Hippos are the most dangerous animal on the continent, responsible for around 500 deaths every year. Some months later, someone from the Ministry came and shot the hippo as it had become a menace. The Tatelos were allowed some of the meat, and we shared it. Its strong flavour is difficult to describe, and I didn't enjoy it. Tough rules regulate the killing and consumption of wild game in Namibia and, generally, it is illegal to kill wild animals within the national park. Some boys at school were fined for killing a rabbit. However, if an animal was causing a threat, special permission could be issued for its slaughter.

During the dry season, elephants presented a real danger as they smelt water in the villages from 20km away. Parents were afraid to send their children off to school in case they encountered a thirsty elephant on the way. Out at Sangwali this was a regular occurrence, and the Ministry deployed experts to scare the elephants away. These experts usually camped out in the problem areas, taking it in turns to set off firecrackers and rifle shots. I once met an elephant while riding my bike on the road to Kanono; I was terrified and overjoyed in equal measure.

Throughout life, most days merge into one another, a haze of work and mundane chores, idle chats and shared jokes with few lasting moments committed to memory. That day out with the Tatelos was a rare day, remembered in detailed, glorious Technicolour, one of those days that stand out and remind you to try and make more of life every day.

Mumbiya and Jude

Mr Tatelo and me

CHAPTER 4
MY FRIDGE

When I announced that I was heading off to do VSO, friends would frequently ask, "What will your house be like?" I was desperate to know myself but had no information other than its location: the village of Chinchimane, 60km from the nearest town of Katima Mulilo in the Zambezi Region of Namibia. Accommodation was the responsibility of individual employers, and there was enormous variation in the standard provided for volunteers throughout the country. There were palatial, colonial-style near mansions; modern town flats; shabby government block bungalows and shacks out in the sticks. Those who landed on their feet were usually gracious at letting more accommodationally-challenged volunteers come to visit for some creature comforts, and often hosted brilliant parties.

VSO listed the basic requirements that our Namibian employers should provide for us in our new homes. They included a bed, mosquito netting and security bars on the windows, a lock on the door, a fridge, a cooker and access to water. This was fairly basic, but few volunteers had everything on the list when they first arrived; in fact, some had no accommodation at all. Most bore this stoically, although VSO folklore has it that one man went home because his house had no TV and I know of a couple who insisted that their house include a spare room. As far as I was concerned, it was difficult to make demands as I was conscious that I was in a country where new friends and colleagues may not have access to the facilities that I had been promised. On the other hand, employers knew what the requirements were when they advertised for a volunteer, and none of them could be deemed luxuries. If we were expected to do a decent job such a long way from home, then maybe it was only fair we were provided with relatively comfortable living conditions.

My first trip to Chinchimane was just an introductory visit; I had already been told that I would have no electricity, no telephone, phone line or mobile phone reception and no running water in the house. However, neither was there any mosquito netting, fridge or cooker. We had been advised to contact VSO's Head Office in Windhoek straight away if our accommodation did not fulfil the stipulated criteria. This was hard to do when the office was over 1,200km away and I had no phone. Perhaps I should have written them a letter. In reality, if your house wasn't up to scratch, the volunteer community would rally round and deal with it themselves. After my first visit, I travelled back to Katima, where I was staying with Anita who continued to make me feel very welcome as I found my feet.

I visited Mr Simataa, (a different Mr Simataa, this one was head of government stores) at the Katima depot, and asked about the equipment for my house. He was very helpful and agreed that I could purchase most of the items myself and be refunded later on. VSO had issued us all with an equipment grant when we first arrived, so I had some ready cash to do this. I bought wire mosquito grills from the hardware store, which Addie and Kees fitted to the windows and doors for me. It was a bit of a faff as we had to borrow a petrol generator to make the drill work. A gas oven had been ordered, and it arrived a few days later along with a large cylinder of gas. Kees said it would be better to keep the gas outside, where there was a lockable metal cage for this purpose, and pipe the gas into the house. I enthusiastically (and as it turned out, rather naively) filled out a job card at the Ministry of Works to request that this be done.

The big issue was the fridge. An electric one had been delivered to the Katima store by mistake and had to be returned. This time a gas one was ordered, and I was told it would arrive in eight weeks. The party line was that if your accommodation wasn't up to scratch, you didn't start work until improvements were made. This seemed churlish, especially as only the principal and the Tatelos had fridges. Most of the other teachers managed without, and I decided I would too, for the time being at least.

Initially, I travelled back to Katima every weekend and stayed at Anita's house. Even so, keeping food fresh for a week was difficult in temperatures of 30^0C. There were a couple of ramshackle shops in the village, but they sold little, and nothing was fresh. It was mostly candles, soap, bags of pasta, rice or maize meal and tins of pilchards. OK for the occasional emergency meal, but nothing more. My neighbours rented out fridge space to the other teachers but said that I could keep a few items in there for free. I would put a carton of UHT milk and occasionally some sausages on a shelf, but there wasn't room for much else. Fruit and vegetables kept well enough for a week in a cool cupboard, and I ate a lot of pasta, rice and tinned sauces.

The eight weeks predicted for the fridge to be delivered turned into ten weeks, then twelve, and I made weekly treks to Mr Simataa's office to check on progress. Every time Kees or Addie went past his workplace, they would pop in and make enquiries too. After weeks of no news, Kees arranged a meeting with Mr Lupalezwi, the minister for education. He simply pointed out that American Peace Corps volunteers didn't need fridges, and he wished we were a little more resilient like them. I felt torn. But life out in the village was a real challenge for me, and having a fridge, as all the other VSO volunteers in Namibia did, would certainly make life easier. I fantasised about cool water and cheese. In the end, one scorching day after a stressful hike, I landed in Mr Simataa's office tired and hungry and burst into tears. He said he felt ashamed that his colleagues' incompetence had made me cry and within a week, perhaps coincidentally, the fridge had arrived. Arrived in

Katima that is; it would be another two months before it was fitted and working in my house.

I went to have a look at the fridge in Bears Furniture Store. It was beautiful and gleaming and absolutely enormous. I would be able to squeeze into it if ever the heat got too unbearable. Addie drove the fridge (or fridge-freezer as it turned out to be) over to my house, and Lynn and Josephine came round to have a look. We sat admiring it for some time and planned all the cool beers, fresh meat and ice-cold watermelon that we would soon enjoy.

VSO insisted that it be fitted by a professional. The job card for the pipe installation that I'd optimistically filled in all those weeks before was still open, so they could do that at the same time. It was another few weeks before a toothless old chap in a jaunty cap arrived to do the work. He bashed such a hole in the wall for the gas piping that my mosquito netting was rendered a little redundant. Mr Tatelo took one look at it, tutted and said, "For sure the snakes will enter here." The pipes were pretty wonky and dangled precariously, but he insisted they were fine. I had to go to work, and he said he would finish the job, and the fridge and cooker would be connected and working by the time I got home. Doubt crept in when I watched him check for any leaks with his lighter, but I brushed that aside and left for work.

Unfortunately, the professional gas installation expert did not seal the pipes properly and left the gas cylinder fully open. So, when I returned home four hours later, it was to a house filled with gas, and a potentially lethal explosion risk as Florence was cooking tea on an open fire in her garden a few feet away. I was absolutely furious and asked Mr Tatelo whether he thought it was part of a campaign to make me give up and go home or, failing that, to kill me. He laughed and said no, that some people were just stupid.

A man called Frik ran the local hardware store, and I asked his advice. He said the only person in Katima he could really recommend was a gas fitter called Kingsley (I can't remember his surname, and now I can only think of Kingsley Shacklebolt, so it's unlikely to come back to me). I took a taxi to his workshop, where he agreed to travel to Chinchimane during the week and do the job. Of course, he didn't turn up. The frustration was that it was impossible to chase anything up once I was in the village. There was a payphone, but it never worked and to make calls on the school's landline (also incredibly unreliable) was very expensive. I went over to

Kingsley's workshop the following Friday afternoon, but the place was closed. I left him some messages, and he eventually got back in touch to say sorry, he had been very busy, but he would definitely drive out this week. My natural positivity and belief in people was being replaced by a more realistic cynicism, so I bought a wad of phone cards, intending to pester him throughout the week. With perfect timing, the school landline packed up that week. So, each afternoon, when lessons finished, I walked over to the inspector's office to use their phone. On Monday I left a message, on Tuesday I spoke to Kingsley, and he said he would be there at 8 a.m. on Wednesday. On Wednesday, I left another message, and on Thursday I spoke to him, and he said he was ill.

The only silver lining was that Josephine had accompanied me on my trips to the inspector's office and had spotted a ripe papaya on the tree in his garden. I was chatting to Mr Mwilima and Precious when I spotted a flash of red out of the corner of my eye; it was Josephine in her killer red dress, frantically signalling for me to keep them occupied as she knocked it down from the tree with a long stick and smuggled it home. That woman was a bad influence!

On Friday I rode back to Katima and asked Mr Tatelo to drop me straight round at Kingsley's workshop. He was as apologetic as ever, and we arranged that I would go there early on Monday morning and he would drive me to Chinchimane and carry out the job. I told him that if he failed to do it this time, I would go elsewhere, although I didn't really have anywhere else to go. Addie drove me over on Monday morning, and predictably, there was no sign of the man. His expressionless secretary informed me he had decided that he did not want to do the job as it was too far away for him to travel. I lost the plot a bit at this point, and the poor lady bore the full brunt of my weeks of wasted time and frustration as I went into glorious rant mode. She was silent throughout, and when I finally finished, she simply shrugged and swivelled away from me on her chair.

Frick suggested another guy named Eddie, who lived in a caravan close to Jane and Carol's house. He said he hadn't mentioned him earlier as he was a bit unreliable. If Kingsley was the *reliable* option, this recommendation did not bode well. I went over to Eddie's shack that weekend, where there was a recognisable whiff of marijuana as I entered the yard – not always the best sign when you're looking for a dependable tradesman. Eddie and his younger brother Kenny were white Namibians who were unique as far as I know in that they had attended the local school instead of being shipped off to boarding school. They knew Lynn from years back, and Kenny was keen to tell me all about his travels in Scotland, which seemed to involve a lot of getting lost and sleeping in muddy ditches. They were handsome and funny and invited me to go fishing with them that afternoon to discuss the job. I was rather smitten and felt quite pleased that Kingsley had been such a nonstarter.

They picked me up from Anita's that afternoon where she clucked around like a mum and made me promise to call her if I got stuck. We drank beers and smoked and idly fished from the banks of the Zambezi all afternoon. We had to keep moving around as Eddie said if you remained still on the bank for too long, a crocodile could fix you in its sights, swim undetected across the river and leap out at you. He rolled up his shorts and showed me an impressive, jagged scar that ran the length of his thigh. Wow. I'd never met anyone with a real animal-attack scar before (my dad has a small one on his calf where a Jack Russell molested him on the way home from work one day, but that absolutely does not count).

We caught a tiger fish and cooked it on a fire back at their house, and they dropped me home at a respectable hour to avoid Anita sending out a search party. Eddie promised to pick me up on Monday morning and drive out to fix the fridge. I was delighted that he seemed intent on doing the work and even more delighted that I had made some exciting and rather dashing new friends.

Eddie was true to his word and collected me in his truck at first light. He drove barefoot and was eating what appeared to be part of a cow's leg. When we arrived at the house, he pulled out the fridge, and to my embarrassment, there was a small poo behind it. Housework has never been my forte, but this was a new low. Jude, or quite possibly Mumbiya, must have deposited it there, some time ago judging by its condition. Eddie was unfazed and kicked it out of the door. "My house sometimes has shit in it too," he said rather worryingly. By the time I got back from work, the job was complete, and my beautiful fridge and cooker were finally connected and in working order. The piping was neatly fixed to the wall, and the giant hole had been filled in. I made Eddie a sandwich, paid him half his money, and arranged to drop by that weekend with the rest of it. I immediately ran over to get the girls, and we ceremoniously stocked the fridge and agreed to meet later for a cool drink. The date was 31st January; it had only taken four months and nineteen days!

Having the fridge meant I could buy a wider range of fresh food from Katima, and I became more adventurous with my cooking. I made spaghetti bolognese, roast beef with Yorkshire pudding, and shepherd's pie for my friends to try. I heard that Mr Chalo's birthday was coming up, so bought some basic baking equipment from the Lucky Joy China shop and attempted to bake him a cake. I had bought a VSO cookbook, put together by volunteers. Most of the quantities were in handfuls and mugfuls, and for anything else I borrowed a balance from the laboratory. The carrot cake turned out pretty well. Mr Chalo begrudgingly shared half with the rest of the staff and took half home. I assumed he would share with his family, but Josephine said he would most likely eat it all himself. He was quite large. Mr Nzwala's birthday was next, and he requested a chocolate cake. Lynn marked everyone's birthday on the calendar, and I agreed to bake a cake each time.

Some of the ladies asked whether I would show them how to bake the cakes and suggested we set up a cooking club. We arranged a get together for the following week.

A lot of people had electric ovens in their homes in town, and Florence had a gas one like mine, next door. However, they said they didn't use them often. Most dishes could be cooked on the hob or on an open fire outside. When accommodation was built in Windhoek to house displaced people, fitted kitchens with basic appliances were included, but no one used them, preferring to cook outside. Lynn said it was more sociable, much cheaper, and a mum could keep an eye on the kids playing outside while she cooked. The baking lessons were great fun, although it was expensive to buy all the ingredients from the supermarket.

The first lesson was for the carrot cake and chocolate cake. Florence, Anntoinette Muhinda (one of the English teachers), Rachel, Josephine, Lynn and an assortment of small children all turned up, so it was a bit of a squeeze. We shared one cake tin, so spent the whole afternoon on task I was a bit worried about the amount of gas we got through, but we agreed that next time we would just bake one and everyone would take it in turns to borrow the recipe and the cake tin. Miss Muhinda borrowed it first, as it was her boyfriend's birthday that weekend. However, she told me it hadn't worked well; the cake had not risen and had a huge hollow in the centre. I asked whether she had opened the oven door at all during cooking. "Yes, of course, Susan, I checked on it every few minutes as I did not want it to burn." I missed that important point from our lesson.

The fridge was so big there was no way I could fill it alone, so Lynn, Josephine and Rachel had a shelf each. This was generally fine, but I sometimes begrudged the trail of people knocking on the door around mealtimes or early into the evening asking for food or cold water. On scorching afternoons, when all I wanted to do was lie sweating on my bed, there would be constant requests for cold water. Pretending that I wasn't in didn't work, my every move was noted. Sometimes I felt like a tagged offender on parole.

The boarding house kitchen used gas for their cookers and fridges too. One day, the school housekeeper turned up at my door asking whether he could borrow my gas cylinder. He said that they had run out and wouldn't be able to cook the student's evening meal. They were expecting a delivery, but it had been delayed. As soon as it arrived, they would replace my cylinder, the following day at the latest. I agreed as I knew things would keep cool until the next day, and it would be horrible for the students to have no tea. I could cook mine on Florence's fire. Needless to say, no gas materialised the next day, and when I wandered over to enquire, I was told that my cylinder had been used up and the delivery had still not arrived. I was worried that the girls' food would get spoilt, so I squeezed it into Mrs Mahoto's fridge. Luckily, there wasn't much.

I disliked the housekeeper; he made me feel uncomfortable and always stood too close when he talked to me. He would shout across the schoolyard "Susan, send me over some of your white friends from England. I want one for a wife." The situation was annoying because I had no gas but more so because it meant I had to talk to him. It was a week before my cylinder was replaced despite deliveries arriving before then. Lynn said it was wrong of them to ask to use my gas; they wouldn't dream of asking Mrs Mahoto or Mr Tatelo for theirs. She said the housekeeper had messed up because he hadn't placed an order at the correct time, and he was too lazy to drive into town to rectify it. She said next time he asked, I must just say no. Rather than making me a soft touch, this volunteering business was turning me into a tough cynic.

I learnt another valuable lesson the first time I switched the fridge off when school broke up for the holidays. I thought I had cleaned it scrupulously, but I must have left a scrap of meat in the freezer section. When I returned a month later and opened the door, a swarm of fat, black flies and the sour tang of meat greeted me. It was gross, and I spent my first night back sleeping on Josephine's floor to avoid the stench.

Cake making with (from left) Rachel, Claire and Josephine

CHAPTER 5

THE BAKKIE

Namibia is a vast country and getting from A to B can be challenging. For long journeys to Rundu or Windhoek I took the Intercape bus, a comfortable coach that ran twice weekly from Cape Town, South Africa to Livingstone, Zambia. Katima to Windhoek took thirteen hours and I made this journey a number of times.

Once I was in my favourite seat – top deck at the front, looking for animals – when we hit a guinea fowl. It pierced the windscreen with its beak and shattered the glass. The elderly man sitting next to me started laughing, pointed to the small hole in the centre of the shattered glass and mimed a gun with his hand. "I thought it was bullet," he said. "I thought it was a second uprising, and we were being shooted." All of the passengers were asked to leave the bus and we ended up sitting by the roadside for eight hours until a replacement coach arrived. Some resourceful young men lit a fire and cooked the unfortunate guinea fowl.

If the Intercape was too expensive or you needed to travel on a day other than Friday or Wednesday, another option was to get a seat in a combi – a small minibus or people carrier. These were privately owned and frequently in a poor state of repair. They would be piled high and driven fast and I rarely travelled this way if I could help it. The newspaper was full of stories of fatal combi crashes. There were regular collisions with other vehicles in the country's busier parts around Oshakati, or collisions with wildlife when driving through the bush. In the newspaper I read a harrowing account of a minibus hitting and killing an elephant calf. The mother, wild with grief, trampled the combi, killing three passengers.

I once took a combi back to Chinchimane with a group of students; I could smell booze on the driver, and he kept weaving along the gravel road. Namibia drives on the left and bordering Angola on the right. Every time he strayed over to the right-hand side of the road, he would laugh and say, "Now we are in Angola," and, "Phew, we are returned home," as he drifted back to the left. The joke rapidly wore thin, and the students were getting scared. I asked whether I could drive the vehicle. He conceded as long as I agreed to marry him. I accepted his proposal and drove along for about twenty minutes before I touched the brakes to make the left turn onto the village track. Nothing. We had been driving with no brakes. Thankfully, we were travelling slowly, but even so, I skidded across the gravel and into the bushes. I yelled at him, in tears and shaking, and we walked the final mile. Needless to say, the marriage was off.

The most common way to travel around the sparsely populated Zambezi region was to hitch a lift, or "hike" as it was called. There were various hiking posts around town, referred to as "stations", and there were particular days and times when you were most likely to enjoy success. Friday afternoon was when people tended to head from the villages into town, and on Sunday afternoon they made the return journey. Bakkies (an Afrikaans name for a pickup truck) would be filled with the weekly shop: sacks of maize meal, bales of toilet roll and clinking carrier bags of beer. Wednesday morning and evening saw regular traffic too, as people made a mid-week trip. I usually got a lift with Mr Tatelo or Mr Nzwala, but sometimes had to hike, which could be nerve-wracking. On a Sunday afternoon, villagers would congregate at the station outside the Happy Joy Joy China shop and wait for a hike back to school. Most people drove bakkies, and to travel in the cab was much safer and quite a privilege. Remaining passengers would pile into the rear of the bakkie and cling on. It was odd that people in the front could be prosecuted for not wearing seat belts, while those exposed in the rear could do what they liked. If a bakkie crashed and rolled, it usually spelt the end for those in the back. I liked travelling in the back, provided the driver went relatively slowly. I enjoyed feeling the wind in my hair and chatting with the other passengers. It felt exciting and reckless, although I'm not sure I'd be quite so up for it these days.

Some of my favourite journeys were shared with a man called David from Linyanti Stores. I had recently finished a booked called *Into Africa* by Martin Dugard, all about Henry Morton Stanley's search for Dr David Livingstone. Livingstone lived in Linyanti for some time and the village was marked on the map at the beginning of the book. There is a wonderful, tiny museum in

Sangwali, full of letters, photographs and artifacts from Livingstone's travels in the Zambezi Region. It was set up by Mr Linus Mukwata and benefited from an EU funded upgrade in 2016. I love it and think it is worth a detour if you are ever in the area. David held Dr Livingstone in high regard and had done research into his life here. He had elaborate plans to add Linyanti to the tourist trail; he wanted to set up guided tours following in Livingstone's footsteps, build a lodge and an extension to the museum. We would spend our dusty journey talking through his plans and getting carried away. It was rare that I bumped into him, but when I did, it was always a real treat. I didn't see any signs of the Livingstone tourist trail on subsequent visits, but I hope David hasn't given up on the dream.

I had a couple of unpleasant hikes, like the time Mr Simataa and I got a lift with a police officer and a bakkie full of confiscated meat. The meat was apparently illegal bush meat, and it was pretty smelly. Travelling with meat was not unusual – I had experienced a kudu leg, dead goat, live goat, chickens and sacks of pungent fish on journeys before. The problem was the speed. The officer drove so fast on the gravel road that I felt sick with fear. The stinking crates slid and crashed into us, and Mr S closed his eyes and prayed. I banged on the cab and indicated to the driver that he should slow down, but he sped up. I banged again, and he skidded to a halt. When I complained that I feared for our lives, he laughed and said we should get out and walk. With only an hour of daylight left, chances are we would've been stranded in the bush overnight. Mr S, silent in prayer up to this point, stated that I was a visiting diplomat from Britain and that if I was killed, it would create international tension. I'm not sure whether the cop believed us, but he did slow down.

I once shared a crowded bakkie with an evangelical preacher who spent the journey denouncing white people and raving about how they impregnated condoms with the HIV virus, then distributed the condoms throughout Africa. He said that whites wanted to confine the Black African to compounds like the natives of America and Australia. I daresay that last point has been true at times in history, but his ranting wore thin after an hour.

Weeks later I met a man called Jarvis at a party. He looked vaguely familiar, and I asked whether we had met before. He told me he had been another passenger during the bakkie tirade. He said he had felt bad for me and had wanted to say something but knew the speaker as a notorious madman known for violent outbursts. Rather worryingly, he was the principal of a local primary school.

One of the worst things about hiking was the lengthy wait for a lift. I would regularly stand at the roadside for over two hours before a vehicle passed. It was most desperate when you could see one coming, but they did not stop. Occasionally, tourists travelled on this road, taking the longer route to Lianshulu Safari Lodge. Tourists rarely offered lifts but would sometimes screech to a halt when they spotted my pink face, maybe assuming I was in trouble. One wealthy-looking white couple had an empty back seat but insisted that they only had room for me. I refused their lift, telling them rather self-righteously that I would wait and travel with my friends. Josephine said, "Susan, you should have gone, now you will need to wait a long time. We are used to being treated like this."

One particularly slow day, I had been waiting for over two hours, and it was getting late. People did not like to drive on the bush roads in the dark; the risk of hitting wildlife was very high. Finally, a bakkie stopped, and we piled in, hot, tired and hungry. Namibian law states that foreign individuals should carry ID with them at all times. If there is a roadblock, the police may ask to see it, and if you cannot produce ID, they can request that you return home to collect it. I had been advised that, in reality, this was unlikely to happen when travelling locally. I didn't want to carry my passport around with me, and I was told that roadblocks didn't occur on small local gravel and sand roads. Late that afternoon, we were pulled up by a group of four police officers and they immediately demanded to see my ID. When I explained that I had left it at home, they told me I must get out of the bakkie and return home to collect it. I would not be allowed to pass without it.

No one else was asked for ID, even though I knew there was a Zimbabwean and a Zambian on board. I was so tired and hungry, and I knew that the chances of me getting a hike back home were slim. I would be stranded at the roadside with the cops until their shift ended, and then there was no guarantee that they would take me back to town with them. Maybe they were looking for a bribe, maybe they were just doing their job, but I decided I would not get out of the bakkie. I explained that I would not be able to reach home, I would give them my details, and there were others here who could vouch for me. They repeated their request a number of times, and I just kept saying, "No, I am not getting out." Neither the driver nor any of the other passengers complained about the delay, and some were telling the officers to let me pass. After about twenty minutes, they gave up and waved us on with a flick of their rifles. From then on, I carried a certified paper copy of my passport wherever I went.

I missed countless meetings in town because I couldn't get there in time and began setting off up to a day before my meeting to ensure I'd make it. I once held a poorly-attended workshop in Chinchimane, only for three teachers to arrive a day late – they had hiked from Sangwali.

To visit the nearby schools of Kanono (5km) and Linyanti (15km) VSO's brilliant idea was to buy me a bike. They also bought me a cycle helmet, as it was a legal requirement to wear one, despite the fact that it was not possible to buy one in Katima. I'd heard that the rule was only really enforced in Windhoek (probably from the same person who had told me I wouldn't get asked for ID). I saw some good helmet improvisations, the best being a hollowed-out half watermelon fastened with string. The first time I cycled to Kanono, I was extremely nervous. Pedalling through sandy gravel under a fierce sun is not easy, and I was wary of encountering a snake. I was also anxious about the packs of feral dogs that loitered on the outskirts of each village. They would chase me, snarling and snapping at my legs. I took to carrying pockets full of stones to pelt them with, a trick I'd learnt from the village children. I was quite a novelty, the *makuwa* on a bike in the middle of nowhere, and I was greeted by shouts of "How far, how far?" whenever I saw someone. "Back home to England," I would reply.

When I arrived at Kanono, it felt like such a momentous achievement that I was disappointed there wasn't more of a fanfare. The lovely Mr Joba fetched me a cup of water and laughed at my red face as I headed to class. The plan was to visit Kanono once a week to team teach some of Mr Joba's practical classes and bring him resources. When I left Namibia for home, Mr Pele Pele (the principal at Kanono) said that he couldn't believe his eyes when he first saw me cycling up to the school gate. He said that no teacher he knew would agree to cycle that distance through sand for work, certainly not a woman. He said I was a strong, brave woman, and he greatly appreciated my effort. I felt like crying and wished he'd said that earlier.

Josephine said that bicycles were for poor men and children, and it's true that I never saw another woman riding one. If I went for a leisurely ride, kids would clamour for a go, and I'd let them take it in turns. Occasionally, male students would ask to borrow the bike, saying they wanted to visit their mum in a neighbouring village or cycle to a church meeting. I always said yes, and in exchange, they would give it a thorough clean, oil and pump up the tyres. Josephine said, "They want it so they can go fuck their girlfriend in Linyanti," which rather dampened my warm, philanthropic glow.

Cycling became less practical once the rainy season began. The mornings grew colder. Not quite frosty, but I could see my breath. I took to wearing a pair of socks on my hands, unable to find gloves for sale anywhere. One day I was halfway to Kanono when it started to rain heavily. The road became a slippery mess, and I was a bedraggled wreck by the time I reached school. Mr Joba had walked part of the way to meet me, becoming worried when it poured, and I was late. He strode up wearing his winter coat with *LAPD Law Enforcer* emblazoned across the chest in gold letters and handed me a flask of hot tea: what a hero. By the time I'd got changed and done some work, the sun was blazing again, and I found myself too hot on the return journey home.

After a year of cycling and hiking, I became fed up with the whole thing and looked into the practicalities of buying a car or bakkie. My work and social life would benefit greatly from improved mobility, and I convinced myself that if I wanted to get the most out of my remaining time in Namibia, I needed a set of wheels. Second-hand vehicles held their value exceptionally well, and as a result were expensive. 4x4s were regularly sold on by departing volunteers, but these were well beyond my price range. In a move not really befitting a thirty-year-old independent adventurer such as myself, I phoned my dad, and asked if I could borrow some money. I did some research (asked Lynn and Mr Tatelo), and it seemed that the most cost-effective option was to buy an ex GRN (Government of the Republic of Namibia) vehicle at auction and do it up. Each regional government department had a variety of cars, pick-ups and trucks used for official business. They were mostly Toyotas and Nissans, except for a fleet of 800 Chevrolets donated by Michael Jackson. Jackson visited Windhoek in 1998 and made a large number of donations to the newly independent nation. Every time we spotted one of the Chevies, Mr Joba would break into a rendition of *Billy Jean* and perform a moonwalk if the situation permitted.

Periodically, a government auction would take place, and old or damaged vehicles were sold. I had no experience of buying and doing up cars, so this was not something I could do alone. Eddie and Kenny agreed to help me. We visited the auction site the night before the sale to identify any potential bargains. I had rather set my sights on one of Jackson's Chevrolets, but sadly there were none for sale that day.

Eddie spotted six bakkies he thought might be worth buying. We weren't allowed to take any for a drive (two of them didn't have wheels anyway) or even start the engines, so it was all a bit of a gamble. All I could do was trust Eddie's judgement.

Mrs Mahoto let me have the day off school to attend, and Kenny came with me for moral support. I had to pay a refundable deposit of N$16,000 (about £800) before I was allowed into the auction site, and any purchases had to be paid for in full, in cash, that same day. I had another N$30,000 strapped to my tummy in a sweaty money belt and I felt pretty nervous. The auction was organised by a slick team from Windhoek, and it kicked off promptly and at a phenomenal pace. Before I'd really grasped the procedure, the first few vehicles had been sold, including one of Eddie's recommendations. The main man was huge and shouted in that characteristic, crazily-fast cadence favoured by auctioneers and horse-race commentators. It was incredibly noisy – there must have been three hundred customers, all men, jostling and crowding around each vehicle as it came up for sale. People were balancing on cabs and one another's shoulders to get a better view. Kenny asked whether I'd like to sit up on his shoulders, which was sweet, but I suspected I was heavier than him and would have been mortified if he'd collapsed under my weight.

I was outbid on five Toyota bakkies, each selling for a few thousand Namibian dollars more than my budget. There was only one more that I would consider buying, and I feared I would go home empty-handed. The bidding on a Nissan Hardbody started low, and I made a bid. Another shout went up, and I bid again. There was a short pause, then, "Going once, going twice, sold to the little white lady," yelled at breakneck speed. Some shouts of complaint started. Apparently, there had been confusion, and bidders had thought the next item was a clapped-out ambulance with no engine, not my Nissan. Kenny said some of the men were angry as they wanted to bid for the Nissan but had thought it was coming up next. Others complained that the exclamation of sold had come too fast. They hadn't had time to outbid me. Three men approached me and offered more than I had paid to buy it off me there and then. The auctioneer just grinned and gave me a theatrical wink. I think the complainants probably had reason to feel put out.

When the furore had subsided, and the crowd moved on, I inspected my new bakkie. It looked battered but, to my eyes, pretty cool. The auction rules were that all vehicles had to be paid for in full and removed from the auction site by nightfall, otherwise, they would be re-sold the following day. I paid my money and filled in the requisite paperwork before being handed the keys. I was told that the registration documents were still in Windhoek but would be delivered to Katima the following week. This turned out to be an enormous lie, and I ended up travelling the 1,200 km to Windhoek myself to collect them. Inevitably, the engine didn't start, and it only had two wheels. I had five hours to find two more wheels and get my new truck towed home.

Eddie resourcefully borrowed some wheels and towed the Nissan to his workshop, where it stayed for the next three months. I bought four re-conditioned tyres from Otjiwarongo and collected them from the Katima Post Office. Eddie fitted a new engine and tried hard but failed to get the diff lock to work. (I've typed that like I know what the diff lock is – something to do with the four-wheel-drive mechanism, apparently.) The fuel gauge was broken and would have cost a fortune to fix, so I got into the habit of checking the mileage and filling up after every 200 km. Eventually, the odometer died too, so I had to note the number of journeys I made, and the rough distance travelled. This was complicated by the fact that I rarely had enough money to fill the tank completely. I frequently misjudged how much fuel I had left, and the bakkie would sputter to a halt, thankfully always in town, so I could walk to the petrol station where I would buy a watering can full of diesel and carry it back to the abandoned truck. It was never the most reliable of vehicles, but it improved my life tremendously.

Mr Malapo borrowing my bike

My bakkie

CHAPTER 6
A WEEKEND IN THE VILLAGE

Thursday afternoons were spent preparing to go to town for the weekend. Lynn called it "beautification time". Most teachers lived away from their partners during the week, housed in accommodation provided by the Ministry of Education. On a Friday, school closed at lunchtime and staff would journey into town to see families, take care of business and stock up on supplies. For schools further out in the bush like Sangwali or the floodplains around Shuckmannsberg, this journey might only take place once or twice a term. When Joso was skint (which was most of the time), she stayed in the village for weeks on end, passing shopping lists onto friends when the cupboards were bare. Most professional families had at least two homes or often three if they were teachers. For example, the Tatelos had their concrete school house next door to mine, a traditional mud and thatch village house on their farmland out near Lianshulu and a town house in Katima. Florence said that she had to buy three of everything and struggled to remember which house she had left items at, including her children.

Payday came at "month end", and at this time, there was a celebratory air, and all the teachers would travel to Katima. No one did any work on the Thursday afternoon of month end; we were all too busy packing and beautifying so we could hit the road the second that the school bell rang. The ladies would braid each other's hair and weave in extensions; Florence always put on her best wig. I felt a bit left out, so Josephine bought me a packet of rollers, and she would pin these into my hair in her back-yard salon. The first time I took them out, she said, "Magnificent, your hair looks like a giant, very enormous bush," and kept patting it and poufing it up. I rather liked it – very Carol Decker circa 1987. I sang a wobbly chorus of *China in Your Hands,* and Joso laughed and said I was a shit singer.

Sometimes we painted our nails from my limited selection of varnish. Josephine and Lynn only ever painted their left hand, saying it was too tricky to do the right and they would make a mess. When I offered to do it for them, they said no. One hand looked good, two was too much, a little showy. I occasionally shaved my legs, which caused quite a stir. Joso tutted and told me the hairs would grow back thicker and pricklier, which, of course, is true. Lynn had shaved one of hers years ago and pointed out how much hairier it was now compared to the other leg. She looked pretty funky with one hand of painted nails and one hairy leg. When we were thirteen, my friend Emily and I ran a razor over part of our arms to see how smooth they felt, and I now have a luxuriantly hairy patch on each arm. I seem to recall Emily did a whole arm. Perhaps asymmetric hairiness is more common than we think. Joso said I should leave my legs to "grow crops," although they'd both sit and idly stroke mine whenever I got around to shaving. I love the aesthetic of a smooth leg but cannot bear the revulsion that an unshaved one seems to cause. In a UK school where I taught, I chatted to a colleague about a Year 8 girl who was struggling to make friends. My fellow female teacher said that the girl needed some support with personal hygiene and that "She really needs to start shaving. Have you seen the thick black hairs on her legs? They are disgusting." The girl we were discussing was twelve years old.

The most time-consuming part of my beautification regime before a trip to relative civilisation was a pedicure. A combination of heat, sand and wearing sandals all the time wreaked havoc with my feet. I developed a hoof, which then started to crack. I could stick a pin some way into the hoof and not feel a thing; its rough surface would get velcroed to the mosquito net at night, leaving me in a panicked tangle. The cracks got ingrained with dirt, and the whole thing looked and felt hideous. My second toe protrudes slightly beyond my big toe, a trait that I apparently share with Madonna, and, according to a Heart Radio piece entitled *What Do Your Feet Say About You*, means I have leadership qualities and am dynamic and resourceful. Who knew? The dynamic protruding toes bore the initial brunt of every stone and rock that I encountered and developed large callouses on the tip. I snipped them off with scissors when they got too big. Lynn said that a snake could be slithering over my foot or a handsome man trying to get my attention underneath the table, and I wouldn't notice. I'm not sure which situation would be most distressing; I suppose it depends on the species of snake.

To avoid missing out on the advances of a handsome man or death by venomous snake bite I developed a foot care plan: I soaked my feet once a week in warm water, which was quite a palaver involving a walk to collect water and then sometimes building a fire to warm the water if my gas was out. After a luxurious soak and exfoliation with a homemade sand and salt scrub, I then attacked them with my imported Body Shop File a Foot; it wasn't really up to the job, and I eventually replaced it with a piece of coarse sandpaper from Bargain Building Supplies. I was perusing the sandpaper aisle when Frick came over and asked what I was looking to sand. When I replied, "My feet," he grinned and said I'd need an electric sander to get rid of my "Africa feet." This ritual just about kept them human, but it was an ongoing battle. My brother sent some peppermint foot soak and intense cracked heel moisturiser through the post. The cream smelt very pungent. I checked the ingredients and found it contained urea, apparently a well-known and effective moisturiser. So now I had a hoof, and it smelt of wee. Years later and I still don't think my feet have fully recovered.

As soon as school finished on a Friday, everyone piled into a bakkie and set off. Most people would reserve a place the day before. Combis arrived from Katima at the end of term to cope with the extra travelling students, and any stragglers took their chances hiking at the side of the road. For the year before I bought my own truck, I usually travelled with Mr Tatelo, squeezed into the front seat with Florence and Mumbiya. Mumbiya would clamber onto my knee and fall asleep; a couple of times she did a little wee on my lap. We listened to the same cassette of Lozi music every journey. When I got my own bakkie, the tape player did not work, and I missed the journey soundtrack. Lynn would sing instead. Our favourite was *African sky blue, will you bless my life?* Occasionally, Mr T gave Mrs Mahoto a lift, and I would be downgraded to the back. I learnt from the other women to wrap a shawl over my head and face when travelling in the back of an open pickup, otherwise, you landed in town a dusty, bedraggled mess. I was frequently ravenous on the journey as fresh food would have run out by Friday, and often the gas too, making it a faff to cook. I was limited in my grocery shopping by what I could physically carry. As a last resort, I would rehydrate a packet of instant noodles in cold water overnight and make do with those when supplies and fuel had run out. Instant noodles featured quite heavily in my Chinchimane diet.

Mr T was a careful driver, and with frequent stops to drop off and pick up new passengers the journey took ages. On arrival in Katima, he would drop me at the OK Superstore where I always bought an enormous piece of prosaically named brown cake (a yummy, stodgy cinnamon and fruit slab) and sat on the step outside the shop to refuel and think through my list of tasks for the afternoon. Back home, one of my guilty pleasures was to gather a selection of tasty nibbles, buy a copy of *Heat* magazine and find a quiet spot to have my fix of trashy gossip. I always felt a bit sordid afterwards, torn between outraged feelings of female solidarity and a shallow desire to look at the *What Were They Thinking!?* fashion pages. I was looking forward to an opportunity to kick the habit. However, when I discovered a copy of the South African version of *Heat* on sale in the supermarket, I didn't think twice before parting with a relatively large amount of cash and settling with my cake and my magazine on the kerb at the side of the road for half an hour's escapism. I didn't care that I hadn't heard of half of the South African celebrities and soon became au fait with Freshlyground, *Days of Our Lives* and Amor

Vittone and Joost van der Westhuizen (the early noughties sub-Saharan equivalent of the Kardashians). You can take the girl out of a capitalist, celebrity-obsessed culture… At month end, I had to walk over to the Ministry of Finance to collect my pay cheque, along with the rest of Katima, it seemed. The queues were long and the process painfully slow, although there was often a good craic as we waited. Once we got our cheques, we had to traipse to the bank at the other end of town to pay them in. The bank at least had air conditioning, but the entire process could take three or four hours. Sometimes, a white Afrikaner would push in and stroll straight to the front of the queue, a throwback to the apartheid era, although I suspect they probably had their own counter back then. Only once did I see the teller send them to the back of the queue. Each month I filled in a form that would ensure my cheque was paid directly into my account to avoid this lengthy routine, and each month this failed to happen. Eventually, after about a year and a half in the country, my bank account was automatically credited, and then I sometimes missed the ritual.

Once I knew my cash was sorted, the next stop was the post office. I had my own PO Box and regularly received mail from thoughtful family and friends. Letters, postcards and small parcels would be in the locked post box outside. Anything larger involved a trip indoors. Queueing in the post office was a more random, stressful experience. The back wall was lined with plastic chairs for elderly people, those with children or anyone feeling a bit tired. Customers could take mental note of their position in the line, then sit down. I didn't realise this to begin with and got into an irate exchange with a large lady pushing in front of me after I waited for ages. Everyone tutted loudly, and the security guard came over to explain the system. They seemed to anticipate trouble as there were always two, armed security guards on duty, each leaning on a rifle by the entrance. During my first Christmas, I was sent so many parcels that I couldn't carry them all and had to get a taxi back to Anita's house. It made a huge difference to know that people at home were thinking of me, and a perfectly timed book or fancy bar of soap could lift me from gloom, particularly in that first year when I was finding my feet. The system seemed pretty secure, and I was only aware of one parcel that failed to arrive.

Occasionally, I chose to stay at the village for the weekend. Sometimes because I didn't have much money left, sometimes because I felt I'd overstayed my welcome kipping at other volunteers' houses and sometimes just because I felt I ought to. I found these weekends challenging. Currently, my life is filled to bursting point with work and the general bustle and mayhem of family life; the thought of a weekend of near isolation with nothing pressing to do sounds like absolute heaven. Who was it who said that solitude is like vodka? A little is bliss, too much and I become uncharacteristically emotional and cry. I had just turned thirty, and my friends back home were getting married and having babies with alarming frequency. I found myself panicking about whether I'd ever fall in love with someone who loved me back, and the ticking of my biological clock seemed incredibly loud out in the Namibian bush. I rarely get enough thinking time these days, but back then, out there, I thought too much. I endlessly questioned whether I was doing the right thing. What about my career? What about babies? What about getting a mortgage? Now that I have all three of those things, I inevitably worry about whether I have enough adventure in my life.

Once everyone had left for town, any remaining staff and students went for a nap. I slept a lot in Chinchimane, longer than I needed to and longer than was good for me.

When I woke up in the cool of the late afternoon, I usually headed back over to school, tidied up the lab or caught up with some marking. My teaching load was light, and the expectations much more realistic than in the UK. Sometimes a group of students would wander over to help. We listened to music and swept and wiped the laboratory. Warm wind and sand blew across the school courtyard and accompanied us into every room. The school and everything in it were permanently dusty. I would sort through the chemical store and make a note of any stocks that were running low. One weekend we painted a giant periodic table on the back wall of the lab. Once students realised I was around for the weekend, there would be a steady stream of requests for help with homework or additional study. Some younger children would knock on the door of my house and announce, "We want to do experiments." Occasionally, I would indulge them and burn tiny pieces of magnesium or set up some rockets with Alka-Seltzer tablets. Sometimes I'm ashamed to say I grumpily sent them away. I found myself torn between craving company and being unable to tolerate social niceties. I was lonely but sometimes found interactions with the villagers exhausting. I was too much on show and found it difficult to relax and be myself. I couldn't understand much of any conversation, and I sometimes felt that I was being made fun of. Looking back, I think I was depressed in those first few months. I wanted someone to talk to, but not someone who would stare at me, openly laugh at me or ask me for money. I missed my old friends, and I thought about what it was to be thirty years old and crying alone in my room with the curtains drawn.

Most of the other teachers went home for weekends. If Josephine was around, I would pop over for a chat, but she seemed to spend most of the time snoozing. It was easy to fall into a pocket of gloom during Chinchimane weekends. Over the years, I have found that the best way for me to deal with low times is to embrace the gloom and have a good old wail and whine, then get busy doing something else. It doesn't matter if you do not know why you're crying; sometimes, you just need to get it out. One village weekend I was in such a pit and indulged in my favourite wailing song: *Something Inside So Strong* by Labi Siffre. I was singing along and having a cathartic weep when I noticed a line of three small faces peeping in at the window, looking bemused. I suspect everyone thought I was bonkers.

I read books posted over from the UK or swapped with other volunteers. Books were hard to come by in Namibia; the nearest bookshop I found was in Windhoek (about 1,200km away), and books were prohibitively expensive. Multiple copies of *Cloud Atlas*, *The Sheltering Desert,* and *We Need to Talk About Kevin* were passed around the VSO community, and ad hoc book clubs would often develop when we all got together. Rachel and Florence borrowed a few and became big Miss Marple fans. I read and reread a diverse mix of old favourites like *Dark Star Safari*, *Notes from a Small Island* and *Bridget Jones's Diary*. Motivated by the latter, I had another failed attempt at *The Famished Road* and *Songs of Enchantment*. My elder brother kept me well supplied with Agatha Christie and Sherlock Holmes novels gathered wholesale from charity shops and sent copies of *Moby Dick* (finished), *Anna Karenina* (nearly finished) and *War and Peace* (abandoned after numerous attempts) for me to battle through. When *Harry Potter and the Deathly Hallows* came out, Mark posted a copy, and with extreme self-control, I didn't open it until my next Chinchimane weekend was scheduled. Then I hunkered down with drawn curtains and read it from cover to cover in bed with three bottles of Tafel Lager and a huge packet of crisps. I ignored some knocking at the door, and it was dark when I emerged from the house; Mr Tatelo said he was worried that I had died. So worried that he hadn't actually done anything. I borrowed teenage romance novels from Mr Chalo's library when I got desperate and particularly enjoyed a reunion with titian-haired Nancy Drew and the handsome Hardy Boys.

I kept vaguely up to date with world news by reading the *Guardian Weekly* (another gift from my big brother: an annual subscription that would arrive, three or four copies at a time crammed into the post box) and listening to the *World Service*. I was usually at least a week or two behind any major news story. It was Mr Tatelo who informed me one morning that we had a new Prime Minister. "Mr Blair, Tony, has gone, and it is now Mr Brown, Gordon. Apparently, restoring trust in politics and winning hearts and minds in the war on terror are his key priorities." I read the papers from cover to cover, even the financial section. Ironically, the time in my life when I had the greatest grasp of financial matters directly correlated with my poorest financial state. I did the crossword and sudoku and then passed the papers on to Mr T.

I wrote letters home full of edited highlights, leaving out the lonely boredom. The *World Service* on the radio was a bit hit and miss. Sunday afternoons were given over to Chinese programmes, broadcast in Mandarin for the large Chinese diaspora settled in Africa. I used to listen to it occasionally, hoping I'd recognise some words. Maybe if I couldn't learn Silozi I could learn Mandarin instead. *Sportsworld* broadcast coverage of premiership football matches at the weekend, something I would normally have no interest in, but I found it rather comforting as I did the washing or worked in the garden. Mostly I listened to local radio stations. They played some music but were primarily public service broadcasts issuing important information and personal messages. There was no mobile phone signal in Chinchimane and only two very unreliable landline phones in the entire village. If a family member became sick or a meeting was organised, the local Silozi station was the most effective way to get a message out there.

iPods were becoming all the rage as I was preparing to leave for Namibia, and I was given one as a farewell gift. My younger brother uploaded his music collection for me (we have similar taste and I hardly ever buy CDs), and I bought a solar-powered charger. I didn't have any speakers, so listening to music was a solitary activity. Sometimes I'd share an earpiece with Josephine, but she wasn't a fan of my music. She said it was too gloomy. Nick Drake, Bob Dylan, Joni Mitchell: she had a point. There is a song I like by David Gray called *Afternoon Debauchery*. It has lyrics about turning on the gas fire and rolling down your tights. It evokes a grey, drizzly afternoon in Yorkshire. Sitting in the dry, scorching sun, I missed a cuddle and some blunt northern humour. I listened to the song twice then gave myself a good talking to. I'd chosen to do this, a choice people living in this village didn't have. I should just bloody well get on with it.

A weekend in the village was a chance to catch up on chores. Clothes and bedding had to be hand-washed, which was quite a task without running water in the house. I am a firm believer in leaving things to soak and had a fairly sluttish attitude to the laundry. I would fill a large plastic bowl with water from the village tap or rainwater in the few months of the year when it rained. I'd sprinkle a generous scoop of OMO washing powder over the dirty clothes, give it a half-hearted swirl around and then leave it overnight. Rachael (my Windhoek volunteer friend) swore by stomping on it barefoot a la grape crushing. I gave this a go, thinking I could kill two birds with one stone and soften my hooves at the same time, but I nearly broke my neck slipping around in the soapy plastic bowl. The big job was rinsing it out the next day. The water would be a repulsive, slimy dark grey, and it took endless trips to the tap to get it to run something approaching clear. Drying was a doddle as even a sodden duvet cover would be dry after a few hours on the washing line. Everything became faded in the sun, and this, combined with the caustic OMO powder made clothes weak and prone to ripping. Joso's boys were always running around with their skinny brown arses hanging out of ripped shorts.

Sand shrouded every surface in my house, particularly during the hottest months when a desert wind would swirl around the village every afternoon. I could set my watch by it. No matter how careful I was about keeping the doors and windows closed and stamping my feet before entering the house, sand crept in through cracks and the many ill-fitting parts of the house. Any microscopic scrap of food left on a kitchen sideboard would attract buzzing flies. These factors forced me to be slightly more diligent with housework than I would ordinarily be. Weekends provided a good opportunity to follow Florence's lead and give everything a vigorous scrub, shake and polish. I wrapped a *shetenga* around my waist, tied a *douk* around my head and set to in a flurry of dust. My enthusiasm waned after about an hour, and the operation could take most of the day, interspersed with generous reading breaks, snoozes and sneaky bottles of Tafel lager. I liked leaning on my broom on the back step chatting to Florence, feeling like a bit like a 1950s housewife, albeit one in the African bush. Sometimes Mumbiya helped out, singing a little song and flitting around with a cloth and ostrich feather duster.

 I had lived in Chinchimane for about eight months when Lynn and Joso took me to one side and said that people around school had started gossiping about me. The talk was that I was too proud and didn't trust anyone enough to let them come into the house and clean it. I was rich and should be spreading my wealth by employing a housekeeper. I was stunned and upset. The thought of employing someone to do my cleaning and washing hadn't even entered my head. Posh, rich people employed housekeepers; busy women juggling hectic careers and kids employed cleaners; gin-swigging colonial ex-pats employed staff. I was none of these and was perfectly capable of keeping my own tiny house clean. My life was far from hectic.

I told them that I would feel uncomfortable employing someone, not because I didn't trust them in my home, but because I didn't like the thought of someone else having to tidy up my mess. Florence and Rachel didn't employ cleaners, but Joso and Lynn did. It seemed that if you were in paid employment, then you were expected to have a cleaner. This was for several reasons: as a sign of status, to save time as you were busy at work, and to spread some of your wealth. I learnt that all of the teachers at school employed a "house boy" or "house girl" who carried out chores around the home. Apparently, these students were not paid in cash, but instead kept supplied with school materials, toiletries, transport and occasionally school fees. It sounded to me like something that might go on amongst the scholarship kids at Eton or Harrow. I would rather pay someone in cash, but the ladies said that the students could not be trusted with cash, and it was better to buy items that they needed.

Rather reluctantly, I agreed to employ a girl to clean the floors, do my washing and help fetch water. I quite enjoyed walking to the village tap to collect water, but seemingly I shouldn't have been doing that for myself either. Joso said, "It is beneath you, Susan. As a teacher, you should not be doing such tasks. People will not respect you if you are collecting your own water." I disagreed but was desperate to try and fit in. I supposed that being flexible and willing to listen, those important VSO attributes I said I had in my interview, also meant I needed to sometimes put aside my own principles and accept those of others. The decision was made, and I asked Joso to suggest someone suitable. She said that one of my grade 12 students, Imenda Sillilo, would be perfect: hardworking, God-fearing and trustworthy. God-fearing wasn't really something I was looking for in an employee, but Joso said it was good as then they knew the Lord would be watching them and wouldn't spend too much time rifling through your stuff or trying to steal things. I asked Josephine if she was God-fearing, and she said, "Me?!" and snorted, which I assumed meant no.

After our lesson that week, I requested Imenda stay behind, and I asked whether she would be willing to do a few small jobs around the house for me. She accepted immediately and said that all of the girls had been hoping to get inside my house to look around; the others would be jealous. She said she would come round on Wednesday afternoon each week.

I did not really know what to do when Wednesday afternoon came around. Should I stay in the house? And do what? Watch? My friend told me that her mum hired a cleaner, and she was forever tidying up before the lady came round because she was embarrassed by the extent of the mess. I did feel inclined to have a tidy up before Imenda arrived. What about handwashing my clothes? Surely not my knickers!? What if I left her to it and she had a rummage through my drawers and cupboards? God-fearing or not, I was sure the temptation to have a quick peek would be too great. I know that would be the first thing I would do.

My main concern was a rather sizeable Anne Summers rampant rabbit vibrator that I had brought over with me. In one of our pre-departure meetings with returned volunteers, I had a chat with a brilliant silver-haired lady in the pub and asked her what travel essentials I should take with me, thinking along the lines of a Tilly hat or a recommended brand of mosquito repellent. I like to pretend that I am an un-shockable woman of the world, but in reality, I am a bit of a prude and I remember going bright red when she whispered in my ear, "without doubt love, a decent vibrator. It will take you a while to get settled, and AIDS is a worry. How old are you? Pushing thirty? You're at your sexual peak, for goodness sake, you'll go mad. But be sure to carry the batteries separately in your luggage or you might cause a security alert." Wise words indeed. Tipsy chats with other female volunteers established that I was not alone in bringing a rampant rabbit with me, but it certainly wasn't something I wanted one of my students to discover. My house was tiny, with little furniture. I had to think of a suitable place to hide a large, bright pink vibrator. Toilet cistern? Too unsanitary. Under the mattress? Too obvious. In the oven? What if I forgot about it and put the oven on and melted it? Of all the things I imagined stressing about when I moved to Chinchimane, this had not been one of them.

I wondered about broaching the subject with Josephine. I knew that she had an open mind as I had been walking past her classroom once and heard her telling her sex-ed class about masturbation in front of a very detailed chalk drawing of the female reproductive system. I decided I would ask her about general protocol for having someone clean your house, but I would keep quiet about the vibrator. I loved Josephine dearly, but I knew she would struggle to keep such a piece of information to herself and would most likely want to borrow it. She advised that yes, I should leave the house when Imenda was cleaning it and that no, I should not get her to wash my underwear. She also said I should leave a strand of hair across any drawers to tell if she had been looking in places where she should not. I saw this in a James Bond film once. Sean Connery tapes a hair across his door and determines that there has been an intruder when he returns to find it broken. Who would have thought that domestic chores would employ such thrilling spy tactics?

When Wednesday afternoon came around, Imenda arrived, and I showed her where I kept the cleaning materials. She was going to sweep, mop, dust and do the laundry, minus pants. I had stashed the rabbit in the bottom of a box of Weetabix. I positioned hairs across some drawers, not because I didn't trust her or particularly minded if she looked in the drawers, but simply to add a bit of intrigue to a fairly dull weekend.

I headed over to the lab and caught up on some schoolwork. It took her ages, and it struck me as slightly ridiculous that I was kicking around, trying to find something to do while she was working hard and cleaning my house. She did a fantastic job, and it was lovely returning to a sparkling home. The hairs had been disturbed, but I couldn't tell whether it was due to prying or they had just been wafted to the floor by a passing broom. I would make a rubbish spy. As previously agreed, I gave her some fruit, paper and pens for school and promised to provide a supply of toiletries when I next went into town. I also gave her my back copies of *Heat* magazine, which she returned a day later, saying that her pastor had told her that they were sinful. God-fearing indeed. I gave them to Josephine instead, who had no such qualms. She read them avidly and generated my first proper nickname from them. It was around the time that Tom Cruise and Katie Holmes had their baby girl, Suri, and there was a section entitled *Where's Baby Suri?* Whenever she was looking for me, Joso took to saying, "Where's Baby Suri?" and it soon caught on. She and Lynn still call me Baby Suri whenever they send a text or email. Years later Lynn got a puppy and named it Suri; I wasn't entirely sure how I felt about that.

Chinchimane village

133

CHAPTER 7
A TYPICAL WORKING DAY

My working day started and ended early in Chinchimane. I set my alarm for 5.30 a.m. and school opened at dawn. Lessons were completed before the midday heat made it too difficult to concentrate. It was chilly at first light, particularly during the rainy season and the Namibian winter. I would light a candle and have a brisk, cold wash. If I really couldn't face that, I would heat a kettle of water on the stove to soften the blow. I had a shower in the house, but the water pressure was never strong enough for any water to flow from it, not even a trickle. My showers were conducted by standing in a large plastic bowl, the one I bought for doing laundry, and pouring water over myself with a jug; hair washing was saved for the weekend. I would use the waste water to flush the loo at the end of the day. Water was carried in a large plastic container the day before from the communal tap in the village or collected in bowls under taps that dripped throughout the night.

Once dressed, I made a cup of tea and stepped out into the yard to greet my neighbour. By this time, Florence would already be up, bundled in hat and coat and heating up a cauldron of water on the fire outside, Jude sprawled at her feet. She kept the fire smouldering overnight, and it never seemed to take much effort to persuade it back to life. I once embarrassed myself by trying to start a fire in the garden on a mildly breezy day. I wanted to emulate Florence's cosy fireside ritual. Despite lots of paper and kindling and a big box of matches, I could not get the thing to take (and I've been on a Ray Mears survival course). It kept blowing out, and I was starting to attract a sniggering crowd. Florence came over and, with her magic powers, had it roaring within seconds. Most families would gather around the pot of hot water in the morning, sleepily washing and drinking tea. My friend Lillian said that the introduction of domestic hot water storage in urban homes destroyed an important social tradition in family life.

Breakfast was a rather European affair: Weetabix with UHT milk, fruit and a slice of bread and peanut butter. I asked Lynn whether there was a traditional Namibian breakfast; the ubiquitous pap replaced Weetabix, but otherwise it was similar.

When I first arrived, Beatrice and Josephine popped round early one morning, interested to see whether I ate anything exotic for breakfast. Lynn said everyone was disappointed to learn it was the same as theirs. Josephine had read in a magazine that Americans started the day with a steak and was rather hoping I did the same. I occasionally made a full English breakfast for my friends at the weekend (minus bacon, which I could never find), and with the Namibian's love of meat it went down extremely well. After breakfast, if I had time, I loved standing on the back step and breathing in the smells, sounds and sights of the village starting its day. Villagers would head out to tend their fields and the air was filled with their shouted greetings: *"Muzuhile," "Mu iketile hande?"* alongside the clang of the cattle bells as the herd boys harried their charges out to find water and better grazing for the day. 70% of Namibians are not in regular paid employment and instead rely on subsistence farming for food and income. Most families had plots surrounding the village where they grew maize, which would be pounded or milled into meal to make pap. The air was dusty, and the sky started to fill with the orange glow of the rising sun. A distant bakkie always turned off the gravel road down the sandy track to school, signalled by clouds of dust. It was Lucy, the secretary from Chinchimane primary school, making her daily commute. Her husband, the fantastically named Mountain (on account of his impressive physique), drove her into work each day from Katima. It must have cost him a fortune in fuel.

At 6.30 a.m., I headed over to school, a stone's throw from my front door. I unlocked the lab, checked my timetable for the day and prepared for any practicals that would be taking place. Most of the students stayed in the boarding house, and they would be up already and getting the classrooms ready. Each morning the rooms had to be swept out as the dust and sand collected on every surface. There was usually a fight to find a broom as they were frequently getting broken or stolen and were only replaced at the start of a new school year. I know some of the more committed class prefects slept with their brooms so they could always fulfil their duty. Bats roosted in all the roof spaces, and their acrid droppings had to be cleaned away. Years later, we had a huge flock of starlings roosting in our garden in Cumbria. Thousands of them would wheel about the sky in an impressive murmuration, then come to rest for the night in our privet hedge and our neighbour's holly tree. All of their droppings produced a pungent scent of ammonia which I found almost appealing. One night I eventually realised why – it reminded me of the smell of the classrooms in Chinchimane.

Lessons started promptly at 7 a.m., heralded by the head boy ringing the school bell. Any latecomers were greeted by a duty member of staff and a swift whack on the palm with a piece of hard rubber piping. This must have been particularly biting on cold hands in the chilly morning weather. I was never put on late duty; I suspect Mrs Mahoto knew I would not be comfortable administering the required punishment. Corporal punishment was made illegal in Namibia in 2001, but its use continued for minor misdemeanours, particularly in isolated rural schools. I asked some of the teachers about this, and they said that generally a blind eye was turned, and most thought it was an effective, immediate punishment; I am sure some in the UK would agree. Some staff used it a lot, others rarely. If my students failed to hand in a piece of work or were late for their lesson, I would keep them in at break time, a standard detention such as I would use at home. This infuriated the young people who were desperate to get the best seats in the dining hall and first pick of the food. I remember a young lad pleading with me, "Miss Ryding, do not keep me inside for so long. Please just beat me and then let me go."

Timekeeping was an issue for staff and students alike as so few people had a watch. A couple of male staff members had one, but most relied on their mobile phones to tell the time. This was fine at the start of the week, but by Wednesday, most had run out of battery, and could not be charged. The only student I knew with a watch was the head boy who was issued with one by the school for his time in office. It was his job to keep time throughout the day and ring the bell at the beginning and end of each lesson. His favourite lessons were often allowed to overrun by ten minutes, and his least favourite were regularly cut short. Occasionally, chaos reigned when a clanging cowbell was mistaken for the school bell and students were dismissed at irregular times. Cows regularly wandered through the schoolyard looking for water and shitting where we stood for assembly. Once, a young bull, tormented by a gang of kids, charged around dangerously, and we all had to stay indoors until Mr Tatelo scared it off by beeping his horn and threatening to shoot it.

We had a break after two, hour-long lessons when the students would head over to the dining hall for their breakfast (doorstop wedges of bread spread thickly with salty butter and a strong cup of tea), and the staff would go home. This was when I would make a filter coffee, buy a couple of fat cakes from Florence and relax in the garden. Lynn and Josephine dashed home to see their babies, breastfeed them and start preparing lunch.

When I arrived in Chinchimane, Lynn was just returning to work after three months on maternity leave. Her gorgeous boy William was cared for during the day by a nanny called Mimi. Mimi was an Angolan refugee who spoke no English and none of the local languages when she arrived. She soon picked up enough words to look for work, and Lynn employed her because she was bright, cheap and William fell in love with her straight away. She somewhat shamed me by learning English, Silozi and some Subeya in the time it took me to mumble through a few greetings. It turned out that Mimi was only fifteen years old and should really have been at school herself. She soon became part of Lynn's family, and the agreement was that when Prince William no longer needed a nanny, Lynn would pay for Mimi to attend school and get some qualifications. By the time she was seventeen, Mimi had a baby of her own and was pregnant with a second, so nothing came of the plan.

Josephine had four children when I arrived and gave birth to a fifth before I returned to England. Her youngest boy, Simataa, and her eldest daughter Katchana lived with her. The middle boys were currently staying with their father in a distant village. Simataa, a solid chunk of a boy, was absolutely terrified of me and would run screaming to his mother whenever he saw me. Josephine said it was because he had never seen a white person before. It took months for him to relax around me, but we eventually became friends. I'm not entirely sure who looked after Simataa while Josephine was at work; sometimes Florence, sometimes Mimi, sometimes one of the students. The young kids could appear rather abandoned to the casual observer, but someone was always watching over them.

Josephine would regularly run home between or sometimes during lessons if she heard her baby crying, give her a quick feed, then dash back. Sometimes she taught with a sleeping babe strapped to her back. When

I was about to go on maternity leave in England, the teenagers in my favourite class suggested I should bring the newborn into school with me. "We can hang a basket from the ceiling, Miss, and we'll help you to look after him." Impractical I know, of course it would be, but I sometimes wish I could have given it a try. Once I was at a teachers' meeting at Masokwatani, discussing moderation of the new exams, when someone passed a squealing babe through the window. One of the headteachers took her, breastfed her, and passed her back out through the window, leading the discussion throughout. No one batted an eyelid. In the UK, women can be lambasted for breastfeeding in a café or on a bus. Lynn said that women had to feed their babies, and they had work to do. If anyone objected to you doing both at the same time, they should be offering to help out instead of complaining.

After break, lessons resumed – three more hour-long classes before lunch. The classrooms were basic; single wooden desks with lifting lids and a redundant space for an inkwell, wooden chairs with metal legs, which were often a tight squeeze for the bigger students. Some of the chairs had no back, which must have been uncomfortable. The students would write or carve their name into their chair and try to keep the same one throughout the school year. Occasionally, small wars broke out when someone sat on the wrong chair, and an indignant youth was left with the backless dregs. The front wall of each classroom was lined with three chalkboards. I was too short to utilise the top part of the board and had to stand on a chair if I had a lot to write. I bought some wedge sandals from Jet to allow an extra sentence or two. I have got used to my interactive whiteboard at school now and can show YouTube clips, amazing photographs and complicated graphs at the click of a button. At Simataa School everything had to be laboriously drawn out onto the board. Writing with chalk is a messy business, and teachers were recognisable by their dusty right sleeves and chalk-stained fingers.

Sometimes we wanted to give the students a test, but the school photocopier and printer rarely had ink, paper and power simultaneously. I was surprised to see a photocopier at all. It worked pretty well if all the stars aligned, and Lynn would set it running of an evening when the diesel generator fired up. The problem was toner; it was incredibly expensive and once it ran out, it wasn't replaced until the next academic year. During one of my pre-departure training workshops, we were shown how to make a copier from trays of gelatine and an ink pen. It was fun to make but ineffectual, and when I suggested to Lynn that we try making one for worksheets, she just laughed. Therefore, most tests had to be copied out onto the board, including accurate graphs and diagrams. This took ages, and sometimes my arm hurt so much I wanted to cry. My right arm developed a small bicep while my left withered. Once I spent ages filling all three boards with some questions about electrostatic forces complete with complicated diagrams depicting configurations of charge, only to discover I had done it in the wrong classroom and Mr Simataa had rubbed them all off.

At around 12.30 p.m. (or whenever the head boy's tummy started rumbling), the lunchtime bell rang out, and everyone traipsed off for a meal and a little lie down. Most staff would cook chicken and pap, which took about an hour to prepare, then would sleep for an hour or so. For the first few weeks, I'd have a quick sandwich or a packet of super noodles, then head back over to school to do some planning or marking. I tried to organise training meetings during this long break, but they were depressingly unsuccessful, and I was usually the only attendee. One afternoon Miss Mushe agreed to meet me at 1 p.m. to practise some experiments. When she hadn't turned up by one thirty, I went over to her house and knocked loudly on the door. She was fast asleep in bed with Mr Sitali. I was really cross. Why would you arrange to meet someone and then go to sleep instead? I woke them up with more knocking, and Precious told me she thought I'd meant the other one o'clock. "In the middle of the night?!" I exclaimed. "Why on earth would I arrange to meet you then? I'll be asleep."

"Well, I am asleep now, and it is too hot to be working. Susan, please go away."

She did have a point; it was scorching. So, I took to having a midday nap, too; I really miss it these days.

By 3 p.m., the worst of the day's heat had passed, and students and staff would drift back over to school after their siesta for sports, revision classes or clubs. I set up a science club, and once a week we met in the afternoon to do some investigations. The most popular were making a solar oven, preparing glue from different hooves (not recommended, very stinky but not very sticky) and testing the strength of bricks made from different ratios of sand and cement. During the rest of the week, I would spend this time planning, marking and preparing equipment for practical lessons. Sometimes I travelled over to Kanono or Lisauli and worked with the teachers there, producing resources, demonstrating how to use equipment or putting a scheme of work together. Once a week I visited the primary school and arranged experiments or activities to the grade 6 and 7 classes. The younger children were less fluent in English and struggled to understand me. I am not sure how useful these sessions were, but the head teacher encouraged me to continue, and I certainly enjoyed them. We would have paper aeroplane flying competitions or explode film canisters filled with water and Alka-Seltzer tablets. It was chaotic, and I worry I left the class rather bewildered.

I admired the headteacher at Chinchimane primary school. Mr Mainga was a clever, kind man, and it was clear that he cared deeply for his students. The school where my Mum works had done some fundraising, and I asked him what we should spend the money on. He was adamant that we should not buy basic school supplies such as books as these must be paid for by the Namibian government. If such essentials were paid for with charitable donations, provision of a decent education could appear cheaper than it really is, and the government would budget accordingly. He said that his country could afford the basics and should not rely on others to educate their kids. He suggested that we used the money to take the children on a school trip, so they could experience the wildlife their country was famous for. He hired a truck and took the whole school on safari into the Mamili National Park. He bought a camera so they could take pictures to show their families on their return. I thought this was a wise and enlightened idea.

I asked Miss Simataa whether she would teach me some Silozi during the afternoons, which she reluctantly agreed to do. Our sessions were rather awkward and went something like this:

Miss Simataa: "What words do you want to learn today?"

Me: "Maybe we could do food today."

Miss Simataa: "What food do you want to know?"

Me: "Well, you know, bread, fish, different fruit, things like that."

Miss Simataa: "Bread is *sinkwa,* fish is *litapi,* orange is *namune* and apple is *apole.* What else do you want to know?"

She once spent two hours teaching me to count in Silozi, which was pretty complicated. I struggled but felt rather proud when I got my head around the system. She finished the session by announcing, "It is a useless way to count, though. No one uses those numbers at all. Even somebody who does not speak English would use the English numbers, not Silozi. Most people who speak Silozi cannot even count in that language." Great use of our time then, Miss! I was a useless pupil, and she was a pretty useless teacher, so the language classes soon fizzled out.

At 5 p.m., students returned to the boarding house or home for their evening meal. Small groups would wander off into the bush, often holding hands. Josephine called this their "special walk," which I initially assumed was code for some sort of romantic liaison. I was startled and rather cheered by the apparently high number of same-sex couples. Turns out a special walk meant they were going for a shit in the bushes. There were toilets in the hostel and in the schoolyard, but with irregular running water, they were of little use. I asked why they didn't dig some pit latrines and got a shrug for a reply. Having a couple of hundred people crap in the bushes on a daily basis didn't seem to cause any detrimental health issues. I suppose the area was big enough, and the weather was conducive to rapid decomposition or desiccation, but it seemed unnecessary and unpleasant. Occasionally, when we were walking or waiting for a hike, a nasty smell drifted over, and Joso would announce that we must have "strayed into the toilette." I started noticing scraps of loo paper flapping on the thorn bushes. The ladies warned me not to go on a special walk myself, it wasn't really the done thing for staff members and I might have an audience. "Catching a glimpse of a white bottom is considered good luck. We are all keen to see the white moon, it might bring us a great fortune, and if it became known that you were squatting in the bush, there would be a guided tour. I would be charging ten dollars to track you." Sometimes I swear Josephine made stuff up to amuse herself and freak me out.

Around this time, I heard about a government initiative to install public toilets in rural villages to reduce the risk of disease. Two cubicles, which looked like the terrifying, self-washing Tardis-style loos you sometimes see in town centres (do they still exist?), appeared in

Masokwatani. They were installed by the roadside, in front of the school, in full view of passing traffic and a focal point for any daydreaming students gazing idly out of the window. Lynn said no one used them because if you were in there for a while, people cheered and clapped when you came out. I don't know whether that is true, but I think they could have been positioned slightly more discreetly.

By six o clock, the sun was setting, and it rapidly turned dark. At 7 p.m., provided the school had enough diesel, the generator's hum signalled the start of evening study. Students were expected to do their homework or extra reading in the classrooms, lit by fluorescent tubes festooned with fluttering insects. This was the time when teachers could charge up their mobile phones and I, my laptop. There was one socket in each room and two in the laboratory. Sometimes there was a queue at each. As we approached exam time, I ran extra revision sessions in the lab for the grade 12 learners. I loved these sessions; the hardest working, most ambitious students would attend. They would ask loads of questions, and we would go through past papers and tackle difficult parts of the syllabus. I encouraged Florence to come to these classes too, although she was usually busy putting Mumbiya to bed.

When there was no generator, evening prep was cancelled, but the keenest students would still turn up, knocking on my door and asking whether we could study by candlelight. I balanced candles in the test tube racks, and we all huddled around the textbook. In the rainy season, a thunderstorm might be raging overhead, the downpour deafening on the corrugated metal roof as we balanced our equations and calculated our moments. Being a teacher can be a stressful, thankless job at times, but those candlelit evening classes were an absolute joy.

The students were generally well-behaved but did not always demonstrate the desperate eagerness to learn that some might imagine. Some were chatty in the lesson, some wandered in late (although the excuses! "Madam, there are elephants on the Sangwali road, we cannot get through"), some regularly failed to do their homework. I remember teachers from home saying, "It will be so great to teach children who really want to learn and appreciate their education." They were teenagers, after all. They had raging hormones and fell in and out of love. They squabbled with their friends, sulking and fighting and taking sides. Their thoughts were occupied with far more than mere study. For many, this village was the extent of their life's experience, but they had ambition and big dreams, and they hoped I would help make them happen. There was a feeling amongst the students that simply having a European teacher would give them an advantage. Lynn said it was exciting too for them to meet someone new and learn about a different part of the world. She fondly remembered an American Peace Corps teacher that she had in grade 11. Mr Simataa and I each taught a grade 12 physical science class, and our results were consistent and similar. I despair when I hear about education volunteering programmes where unqualified European and American volunteers "teach" in an African classroom for a week or two as part of their holiday.

Sometimes we had a night off, and some of the teachers and I would head over to the lab with my laptop to watch a DVD. It was tricky for everyone to get a good view, so we would shuffle seats partway through. I had quite an eclectic DVD selection: some episodes of *Foyle's War*, *Rosemary and Thyme* and *Hetty Wainthrop Investigates* (Mum got these free in the paper and posted them out to me), the first series of *Lost* (box set posted out by my friend Dr Rachael) and the occasional knock-off pirate copy of a film imported from China and for sale in Katima. I think I saw *Brokeback Mountain* in Chinchimane before it was on general release in the UK.

By 9 p.m., the generator would be switched off, and the school plunged into darkness. I walked home, remembering to stamp my feet loudly like Florence had taught me just in case any snakes were loitering. I sometimes listened to the radio for a bit or read using my head torch, but rarely stayed up much later. I liked to lie in bed next to the open window letting a gorgeous warm breeze drift through the mosquito net, listening to the sounds of the Namibian night: croaking bullfrogs, ringing bell frogs, screeching owls, and howling dogs. I slept like a baby in that place.

Mrs Mahoto and grade 12 students

Cows in the school yard

CHAPTER 8
KEEPING HEALTHY

During my first weeks and months, I had to psychologically and physically adapt to my new home. The change in diet and change in temperature had an immediate and disquieting effect on my body. I didn't have a period for eight months, and I developed angry red spots on my neck and face. Miss Mushe kept pointing them out. "These pimples are very bad, Susan." I drew the line when she started to count them. I did one reluctant poo a week despite consuming large amounts of fruit and three Weetabix every day. When I got the chance to meet up with other volunteers, they complained of similar experiences. The impact on our digestive systems was so startling and uniform that it was a regular topic of conservation – not something I would usually choose to discuss with anyone, let alone new acquaintances. Patricia and I referred to our various movements, or lack of, as "le shits grandes" and "le shits petites" (on one occasion "le shits extraordinaire") and would text weekly updates. I wonder what subtle changes my hormones were reacting to that created these effects.

Since returning home, I have researched this, and by research, I mean Googled, "Why does moving to a foreign country affect how often I poo?" In terms of evolution, it makes sense for animals experiencing stress in a new environment to leave as few indicators of their presence as possible. I particularly enjoyed reading the webpage entitled *The Anatomy of a Bowel Movement* with its diagrammatic flow chart and far too much information. The condition is termed "traveller's constipation" and apparently arises due to a change in diet, stress, dehydration, or anxiety about using foreign toilets. I don't think I suffer from the latter but was certainly experiencing all of the other factors in those first few months. However, with limited water, few public loos and having to spend hours waiting by the roadside for a lift, it was actually quite a blessing. When activities finally returned to schedule, I felt rather inconvenienced.

The delay in my periods was also helpful as it gave me some time to think about how I would dispose of sanitary waste while living out in the village. Any rubbish I generated was thrown into a pit that had been dug outside the yard fence. Every few weeks I would set fire to the waste, and anything remaining in the ashes was buried under the next refuse pile. This was standard procedure in the village. All my neighbours had their own pits, and the school had three really deep ones behind the science lab – quite a hazard if you were walking around in the dark. There were weekly refuse collections in town, where waste was taken to the local dump, but not in rural areas. Rubbish pits were popular places for young kids to hang out. They foraged for bottles, cardboard boxes, and empty sacks to play games with. I once lobbed an empty tin into my pit and heard a squeal; three small boys and a dog grinned up at me. Playing with rubbish is not the preserve of the poor; my husband has fond memories of wearing crisp packet gauntlets so he and his chums could pick nettles and do battle, and I spent many happy hours with my brothers scavenging, womble-like, for treasure in the trees behind our house.

Florence said that my rubbish pit was the premier one in the village as I had exotic waste like shampoo bottles and cereal boxes. I didn't want to throw sanitary towels and tampons into the rubbish pit, because even if I wrapped them up, kids would find them, or starving dogs would eat them. They certainly couldn't go down the loo. I wouldn't dream of doing that back home, and my loo in Chinchimane was only flushed once a day using wastewater. If the toilet got blocked, it would most likely be permanent. I asked the volunteers from Rundu what they did, and they introduced me to the moon cup, a small, flexible, plastic device that you push into your vagina. Menstrual blood collects inside it, then you can wash it out and use it again. It sounded eco-friendly, right on and perfect, but I wasn't sure I really wanted to use one with such a limited water supply. Plus, I didn't think that the Happy Joy Joy China shop sold moon cups. I talked to Josephine and Lynn to get the local angle. They said that poorer women would make sanitary pads from old rags and wash them out. Those who could afford it would buy towels and tampons in town and burn them at the end of their period.

This sounded like a better option for me. I would collect everything up in a bag, build a roaring fire (having invested in some firelighters) and plonk them on. It was difficult for me to do anything discreetly in Chinchimane, but I managed to have my little period pyre in the dark at night without interruption. It felt rather ceremonial, like I should have smeared blood on my face and danced around the fire naked and howling. Josephine said that in the past when a young girl first got her period she was sent to the outskirts of the village to stay in a hut on her own. This sounded cruel to me, and the practice is now banned. Josephine said it was a good idea, that it gave young women a chance to learn how to deal with their monthly bleeding when there was little precious water and no sanitary equipment. She wouldn't have to worry about boys making fun of her if blood leaked onto her clothes. Her friends and female relatives would visit with tasty food. She said that it still happened in some communities and was more common over the river in Zambia.

One weekend, we were having a drink at the Zambezi River Lodge and heard raucous singing and music drifting across from Sesheke. Joso said it sounded like the celebrations that took place once a girl returned to the village having experienced her first menstruation: now she was a woman. It made me want to invite everyone round for a singsong next time I lit my monthly fire. In Namibia, at the moment, there is a campaign to make sanitary products readily available to girls and young women. A study by Human Rights Watch estimated that 1 in 10 young women in sub-Saharan Africa do not attend school at all during their period. Here in the UK, we have finally axed VAT on tampons, which was paid because they had, until 2020, been classed as non-essential luxury goods. I was interested to learn that edible sugar flowers and private jet maintenance are not considered luxurious non-essentials – no added tax there. It is estimated that scrapping the tampon tax will save women around £40 throughout their life, so not a life-changing amount. Maybe we should all donate this windfall to a period poverty charity.

When discussing health in Namibia, you cannot avoid talking about HIV. The biggest cause of illness and death in Namibia at this time was HIV and AIDS, and it ranks among the top five most AIDS affected countries in the world. The Zambezi Region was the most affected area in the country, where 42% of the population were infected when I moved there. This was a startling statistic: over 40% of my new friends and their families would be living with HIV or AIDS. I wondered what this would mean for day-to-day life.

My first encounter with the impact of AIDS was in January, four months after my arrival. I returned to Chinchimane from Christmas break and was ushered into the staff room with the other teachers to register students at the start of the new academic year. We were all given a list of names, and our job was to collect school fees or verify exemption. State education in Namibia is free and theoretically available to all, but pupils must pay a small contribution towards equipment such as paper and textbooks. Orphans were exempt from this payment, and those who had lost one parent paid a reduced amount. In 2006, it was estimated that 118,000 children were orphaned due to HIV – nearly 6% of the population. Close to 17% had lost at least one parent.

I was given a list of names from Kapata to Muluti, and there was already a queue of children when I sat down. I watched Mr Chalo and copied what he did. The procedure was to call the child, who was usually unaccompanied, up to the desk and ask their name. I would then tick if they paid their school fees in full, register them on the school roll and send them over to Lynn, who collected the money. If they had lost one parent or were orphans, they needed to show death certificates and would then be exempt from the fee. I found it really difficult to recognise some of the names, and I could tell that the younger children, in particular, found it hard to understand my accent. I could hear Mr Malapo over by the door directing students to my table by shouting, "Over there, the *makuwa* will register you." One small boy looked far too little to be joining secondary school. He was shy, and I could hardly hear him. When I asked if he had his school fees, he shook his head and wouldn't look at me. I asked him whether he was an orphan, and he shrugged. I wondered whether he had understood me. I asked again and his eyes welled up with tears.

I turned to Mr Chalo for help, and he spoke to the boy in English. "Are you an orphan?"

"Yes, my mother is dead."

"What about the father? Is he dead too? You must show the *makuwa* your papers if they are dead."

The boy was clearly trying not to cry and was confused and seemed to have no papers or cash on him. Mr Chalo spoke to him in Silozi, and the boy said something quietly in reply, tears spilling down his cheeks. Mr Chalo ushered him over to Lynn and motioned to a chair at the side of the room. He sat down, looking miserable, and I wanted to hug him. I smiled at him whenever he caught my eye, but he never smiled back. I started working through the rest of my growing line; most were straightforward, and I recognised many students from the previous term.

When I got a moment, I waved Lynn over from the other side of the room to find out what had happened to the small boy. I offered to pay his school fees myself. She said if it became known that I had paid his school fees, I might be inundated with sob stories and requests for money. It was important to speak to a family member first as they may just be trying to cheat the system. This hadn't occurred to me; I am naive at times. Lynn spoke to a few people and tracked down his grandmother, who was sitting underneath the jacaranda tree. I never got the full story but the lad, Simasiku, was in my grade 8 science class the following week, so the matter was clearly resolved without my intervention. I maintained a soft spot for Simasiku throughout the two years I spent in Chinchimane and probably freaked him out by hovering over his desk all the time and constantly grinning at him.

Around the world, there is still stigma attached to being HIV-positive; it was no different in Namibia, and people did not openly discuss their status. It was often possible to determine those who had developed AIDS. I met many people who were painfully thin, exhausted and off work a lot. They would then appear a few weeks later, miraculously glowing, chubby and full of beans. Guillermo, Lynn's boyfriend, said that the usual pattern was that people did not know they had the virus until AIDS developed. They would then go through a period of great sickness as their immune system came under attack and usually visited the local traditional healer or witch doctor for treatment. In rural communities, people will turn to traditional remedies before conventional medicine, and even well-educated people were known to remove a sick relative from the hospital to visit a healer. Remedies mostly involved dried plant roots, leaves and bark; ingested or rubbed into cuts on the body. I asked Lynn about various treatments, and she said, "You name it, someone might use it for healing."

When a casualty was at death's door, as a last resort a family member might take them to the village clinic or

Katima hospital where swift diagnosis and the prescription of anti-retro viral (ART) drugs would almost immediately reduce the amount of replicating virus cells. This had an instant effect on the immune system, and within days improvements were visible. It is estimated that 250,000 HIV-positive people in Namibia are on anti-retroviral drugs. The drugs are expensive and need to be taken correctly to be effective. The Namibian government has made a huge commitment to tackling the issue. Innovative organisations such as Ombetja Yehinga (OYO) were set up to educate young people about sexual health, alcohol abuse, drug abuse, stigma and discrimination through writing, dance, drama and visual arts. Their methods were far more radical than I imagine most would expect from a sub-Saharan country tackling an AIDS crisis. OYO's travelling drama troupes visited schools to talk to young people, and VSO provided fundraising and youth work expertise.

A Christian group came to Chinchimane and put on a play to encourage young people to abstain from sex and avoid alcohol as this led to reckless decision making. Unfortunately, this particular play's main HIV-positive protagonist was a funny, charming man who appeared to be leading a fun-filled and carefree life. His HIV-free pals were dull goody-goodies who did nothing but grumble and endlessly pray. By the end, I thought I would rather be HIV-positive and happy than virus-free and dreary. I'm not sure that this was the message they were trying to get across. The main guy's catchphrase was, "Take it easy bro, everything will be alright," and I heard the kids copying this for weeks after. The play introduced me to the wonderful verb "to condomise", as in "be wise, condomise". Despite the dodgy play, Namibia is seeing success in reducing the prevalence of HIV and AIDS.

Between 2005 and 2013, there was a 36% reduction in new infections, over 8,000 fewer AIDS-related deaths and a reduction in the rate of mother-to-child transmission to less than 4%. I think that's pretty impressive for a less economically developed country with such a disparate and dispersed population. The primary cause of this success has been the government's decision to rapidly scale up its provision of ART services. 84% of eligible adults and 82% of eligible children receive ART. This is one of the highest provisions in the world amongst low- and middle-income countries. The national goal for 2015, set according to World Health Organisation guidelines, was to treat around 80% of those in need. The global treatment coverage currently stands at 65% and only twelve countries, including Namibia, have met the target.

One Friday, a local family asked whether I would take a man to hospital, and I agreed. He could barely walk and had to be helped to get up into the cab. I had never met anyone so thin, and he was clearly in pain. He was probably in his late twenties and sat hunched over in the cab with a woman who I presumed to be his mum. He struggled to talk, and his breath was laboured. Over the previous few weeks, I had been having some trouble with the bakkie; it would splutter and occasionally cut out, but always sprang back to life. I was skint, so had done nothing about trying to get it fixed. On this day, about thirty-five minutes into our journey and miles from the nearest village, the engine spluttered and died and would not start again.

The man was quietly groaning as I sprung the bonnet and peered inside, waiting for inspiration. My other passengers gathered around and offered various solutions. The sick man wound down the window and whispered some advice. He reckoned the fuel pipe was probably blocked with sand; apparently a common problem out here and one I should've picked up from the symptoms over the past month. We needed to attach a hose to the fuel pipe and suck up some fuel and hopefully the sand too, and get things moving again. He whispered instructions, and I sucked up a gritty mouthful of diesel and spat it out. I tried this a few times, but it had no effect, and the bakkie refused to start. I could see that the guy was getting uncomfortable, but there was nothing we could do but hope that someone would drive past.

Incontinence is a common effect of advanced AIDS, and he urinated and defecated before he realised what was happening. I idiotically fussed around, loudly proclaiming that it really didn't matter, not to worry, no harm done. His poor mum looked so sad. Some male passengers took him into the bush to clean up, and I put a blanket over the seat. Thankfully, after about two hours stranded by the roadside, Mountain drove past in his lemon-yellow truck and agreed to tow the bakkie into town. The rope I had was, well, rather ropey, but it did the trick. Mountain drove too fast for my liking and charged me a fortune due to additional fuel consumption, but we eventually made it to Katima. We unhitched at the garage near Eddie's place, and Mountain agreed to drop the man at the hospital. I waved goodbye and wished that I had asked his name.

Katima hospital was the only one in a 300-mile radius, and people living in remote villages had vast distances to travel if they needed medical help. Pregnant mothers approaching their due date would often travel to town and stay with relatives or camp out around the hospital in case of complications. In the New Era newspaper, I recently read about a permanent hostel built outside a hospital in Oshakati to temporarily house expectant mums. A few weeks after I arrived in Chinchimane, a woman gave birth to triplets in the village; mum and all three babies were well and singing in church rang out all day to celebrate the miracle.

I have two sons, and both were delivered by emergency caesarean section. The second in particular was "brutal", according to my midwife. I developed a Bandl's ring, the name given to a constrictive thickening of the uterus's upper and lower segments. Obstructed labour is the most common cause of neonatal death in less economically-developed countries. It is sobering to think that if I had tried to give birth out in the village, both my baby and I would most likely have died. I am a big fan of a mother's right to choose how she would like to give birth, and I know plenty who have experienced successful home births (although the mess!). I wonder how many would risk it without the safety net of a hospital down the road. There is a wonderful charity called Maternity Worldwide aimed at providing support to expectant mothers; one of their goals is to train rural midwives to recognise the signs of obstructed labour early so that a pregnant mum can get to the hospital in plenty of time. They also have stretchers on bicycles for those places that cannot easily be accessed by road, and fleets of heroic midwives on bikes.

Chinchimane was a relatively big village, and we were lucky to have a health centre. There was no doctor, but regular clinics were run by two handsome nurses. They were friends of Lynn's and would come over to chat in the evenings. They organised vaccination programmes, HIV testing, post and antenatal check-ups and gave general health advice. One day, young children were queueing along the church's sandy track, past the primary school and up to the clinic door. There were not that many children in the village, so they must have come from surrounding villages too. Joso said it was polio vaccination day, and everyone was waiting in line for their turn. Polio is one of the few vaccines that can be given orally; most are destroyed by our stomach acid and need to be administered intravenously. No expensive, sterile needles, just a couple of drops on the tongue. I remember being given it in a sugar lump as a child.

I am dismayed by the anti-vaccine rhetoric we encounter on social media, echoed by some pupils I teach and, more worryingly, some colleagues. I wonder if we had to walk for miles and queue for hours, we might value vaccines a little more. A greater understanding of risk and the difference between correlation, causation, and coincidence is needed. This is a job for us science teachers; I hope we're up to it. UK vaccination rates are falling, and a meme (there's a word I hadn't encountered when I started writing this book) is doing the rounds on Facebook amongst my Namibian friends, stating that "the flu jab is a way of spreading cancer amongst the nation."

Whenever I despair of the human race and what the future holds for us, I like to read about the World Health Organisation (WHO) eradication of smallpox. It reminds me of what we are capable of with shared intelligence, compassion and perseverance. It is over forty years since the 33rd World Health Assembly declared, "the world

and all its peoples have won freedom from smallpox."
The Smallpox Eradication Programme began in 1966
with mass vaccination. Campaigns, surveillance and
prevention education were combined to contain
epidemic outbreaks. Intrepid workers in the field
travelled to remote settlements on foot, finding and
treating anyone in close contact with an infected person
and vaccinating those in a radius around. The last known
case was in Somalia in 1977.

In theory, today's social media network should make
such a goal easier to achieve, but the dogged spread of
misinformation is a formidable barrier. There has been
triumphant progress with the eradication of polio.
Nigeria reported its last case in 2016, and four years
later, the WHO declared Africa free from wild polio
after "decades of work by a coalition of international
health bodies, national and local governments,
community volunteers and survivors." Afghanistan and
Pakistan remain the only countries where the disease is
still endemic. Politics and war are the obstacles here, not
science and will.

Around the time I was in Chinchimane there was a local
scandal in rural health centres, as they had apparently
been distributing out-of-date contraceptive pills,

resulting in a number of unwanted pregnancies. Lynn and Joso said they had been donated from other countries. Access to contraception was on the increase but abortion on demand is currently illegal in Namibia. Every year, hundreds of vulnerable women take matters into their own hands and attempt DIY abortions using a frightening array of chemicals, pills and backstreet methods. Some weeks before, I had been reading in the newspaper about the growing number of abandoned babies in Namibia and gruesome discoveries of foetuses and newborn remains found in Windhoek sewage systems. Abortion legislation was inherited from South Africa at independence and only allows a termination in cases of serious threat to maternal or foetal health, or when the pregnancy resulted from rape or incest. I wonder where the burden of proof lies for this. South Africa changed its law in 1997 with the introduction of the Choice on Termination of Pregnancy Act, providing abortion on demand for a variety of cases, free of charge, at certain state hospitals and clinics. Namibian women could pay a few thousand Namibian dollars for a termination in South Africa, but the poorest women in the worst circumstances would be on their own.

Thankfully, I never had cause to go to Katima hospital as a patient, although I visited friends there several times. It was a single-storey, sprawling complex and the only hospital servicing the entire Zambezi Region. At the time, it relied on a combination of foreign-trained Namibian doctors and nurses (usually qualifying in South Africa), Cuban doctors and the occasional aid worker or volunteer. Since 1963, Cuba has been sending medical personnel overseas as part of its foreign policy of supporting anti-colonial struggles. They currently provide more doctors and nurses to less economically-developed countries than all G8 countries combined. There was a vibrant Cuban community based in the compound around the hospital and regular salsa nights in town. I had a brief and delightful fling with a doctor from Santiago de Cuba, who kept a photograph of Fidel Castro above his bed. Hugo was the only anaesthetist in town, and I did wonder what would happen in the event of a surgical emergency on a Saturday night, as we drank rum with sugar and he taught me to salsa in the sand.

A British junior doctor came over for six weeks as part of his elective, and he stayed at Lynn's house near town. Dave had dark wavy hair, a chiselled jaw and piercing blue eyes. He was handsome and rather short, and every time we spoke of him, Lynn and Josephine would tut, "That man needs to be taller. So perfect if he could grow a little." Josephine hypothesised at length that he must have been malnourished as a boy. Dave said that he was impressed with how the hospital was run, although their resources were hugely stretched. He told a great story about how one day he was in the office chatting to the registrar when he spotted a strange creature wrapped in a towel, sitting on top of the filing cabinet. A fisherman had found it injured by the Zambezi banks and wondered whether anyone at the hospital could help it. Dave said he thought it was a seal. From his description and the fact that seals are marine mammals and Katima is about as far from the sea as it is possible to get, I think it was more likely to be an otter. Zambezi otters are big. I doubt he expected to encounter a seal or an otter on top of a filing cabinet in a hospital, but he seemed to take it in his stride. My suspicion was that someone would probably end up eating it.

The first time I visited the hospital was when Rachel and Mr Simataa's daughter, Claire, got badly burned. She had stepped over a lit candle, and her nightie went up in flames, burning her thighs and tummy. In his usual sympathetic way, Mr S blamed Rachel for the incident, saying that she should use the electric lights in their town house, not leave candles lying around. Of course, he gave her no money for electricity, so candles were the only option. Such accidents were common. Houses with grass roofs, candles as the primary source of light and lots of small kids running about made for a high-risk environment. A little girl in Kanono had nearly died the week before when the roof of their house caught fire, and part of it fell on her head as she slept.

Claire was in a lot of pain, and to make matters worse, a trainee nurse had cocked up her dressing, and cotton wool fibres were now embedded in the weeping skin. I charged my laptop and took it round to try to cheer her up. We looked at photographs and a DVD of cartoons. I took her a parcel of food, including lots of sugary treats. No food, bedding or washing materials were supplied by the hospital. Patients relied on friends and family to look after them during their stay, as only their medical needs were met by staff. The ward was relatively small and contained eight beds with a faded curtain between each one. The curtains were all open when I arrived, and a few other kids came over to see what we were doing. I was laughingly told off by the matron for sitting on the bed –

she actually smacked my bottom – but I snuck back on when she left.

At the far end of the ward, a woman was curled on her bed, softly moaning. An older lady held her hand and stroked her hair. It was only as I was leaving that I noticed a shape underneath her bed. It was her dead baby. I had never seen a dead body before, and it really shook me. I can picture that little form now, all these years later.

Lynn and me

Josephine and me

178

CHAPTER 9
KEEP FIT

I am not blessed with youthful looks, and throughout my life people have usually assumed that I am older than I am. This was great when I was doing my GCSEs and trying to sneak into Manhattan's nightclub in Southport. It is less great as the years tick by. During my thirtieth birthday celebrations, a barman guessed that I was forty. No amount of soothing by friends could undo the damage and the celebrations ended with me in a heap outside in a haze of booze-fuelled sobs, contemplating my biological clock.

On a holiday flight with my friend Patricia, who is three years my junior, the Kenyan man sitting next to me asked whether the lovely Patricia was my daughter. Speechless, I turned my back on him before once again hitting the gin. Perhaps it's the drink that has aged me. I was, therefore, over the moon when the Namibians I met mistook me for someone much younger. An eighteen-year-old, in fact! This was marvellous considering I was twenty-nine at the time. One old woman in the village guessed I was eleven years old! God knows what she thought I was doing living on my own and working as a teacher.

When I was introduced to the teaching staff, Josephine said they were all complaining, "Why have they sent us a child?" She said it was because they hadn't met many white people before. I was short and skinny (when I arrived, at least – it didn't last), and "wearing a flowery dress made for a little girl." I was miffed by the dress comment; I had put thought into that outfit and had been aiming for an air of caring authority. As I put a bit of weight on in the first stressful months, the reality of my age became apparent to my colleagues. "Susan, now you are getting fat, and you also look much older." Mr Tatelo said that it was your figure rather than your face that determined how old you looked. He had the figure of a five-month-pregnant woman, so I'm really not sure where that left his theory. He told Lynn that it was difficult to guess a woman's age by looking at her face.

"I need to see the chest area to properly gauge," he said, enthusiastically indicating breasts with both hands. Nice try Mr T.

The food I ate in Namibia was immensely carb and sugar rich, so I inevitably began to pile on a few pounds, something I hadn't really anticipated. I moved to the continent stereotyped in the west by famine and put weight on – typical. I knew action was needed when Josephine announced one morning, "Sue, you are getting fat; everyone in the staffroom is gossiping about it."

"Er, I don't think I'm really getting fat; maybe I've just put a tiny bit of weight on. My clothes still fit me."

"Believe me, you are fat. You just feel thin because right now you are hungry, but when you have eaten, you will know the truth. And your clothes, they are made from stretchy material." She twanged the waistband of my skirt for emphasis.

Blimey, never talk to Josephine if you are feeling self-conscious about your size! I'd like to point out here that I wasn't the only one subjected to weight scrutiny. Everyone was open and honest about acquaintances' fluctuating size. I had been told by some of the other volunteers that to be called fat was a compliment here, recognition that you were wealthy, healthy and well fed. That may have been true for the previous generation, but now it was what it was. If someone told you that you were getting fat, it was most likely because you were, and they just wanted to point it out to you. Ideals of the western body beautiful had spread, and skinny was the new fat in Namibia.

One of the things that I found most frustrating about my new life was the lack of opportunity to take exercise and therefore lose that much gossiped about fat. Even going for a walk was a challenge. Chinchimane was small and crisscrossed by a network of sandy paths. If I attempted to take a walk around the village, I would soon have a gang of small children following me shouting, "*Makuwa! Makuwa!*" or later on, when I was better known, "Susan! Susan!" Some would try to hold my hand, and others would ask for sweets or balloons. Sometimes, I would find this endearing and enjoyed the attention. At other times, I simply wanted some peace and got pretty grumpy. One day a gang of kids yelled, "Give us dollar," and surrounded me. Their gran chased them away with a broom and yelled at them. "How dare you ask the teacher for money? You are not beggars."

She gave me a mango with one hand as she swept away children with the other.

Occasionally, an amorous young man would accompany me on my walks, telling me that my arrival in the village was front-page news, how beautiful I was and had I ever thought about marrying a Namibian man. If I was irritable back home in England, a walk would often be just the thing to lift my mood. In Chinchimane, it could do the opposite as the heat, sand and unwanted attention stressed me out even more. The distances were short and to stray further off the paths or into the bush on my own was dangerous due to wildlife. Lynn and Josephine would sometimes accompany me, which kept the kids at bay, but they walked so slowly that it really didn't feel like exercise at all. I could go out on my bike but again, the options were limited: turn left to Linyanti or right to Kanono and expect a lot of attention en route.

Lynn suggested that we all go jogging, which sounded promising, but when they both turned up in skirts and bejewelled plastic flip flops, I sensed it would not be a rigorous workout. The pair of them ran like tipsy women frantically trying to catch a bus: short, flailing bursts followed by much panting and grasping each other for support. It was fantastic fun, but I probably burned more calories hanging my washing on the line. Over the years since I have returned to the UK, I have taken up running; evolving from "walk a minute, jog a minute" to entering a marathon. I wish I had persevered with running in Chinchimane; it would have made a huge positive impact on my mental and physical health. Although perhaps the risk of being chased and mauled by a pack of feral dogs would have cancelled out any benefit.

The weekends were more active if I travelled to Katima, as I walked around town or took the dogs out with Jane and Carol. They also had a Davina McCall keep fit DVD called the *Power of Three,* which we sometimes did before treating ourselves to pie and chips from the OK Superstore. I asked Mum if she could send me something similar, and a few weeks later, Davina's *Total Body Workout* landed in my post box. My plan was to charge the laptop when the generator was on and do the routine a couple of times a week, at home, with the curtains drawn. I was ten minutes into my first set of exercises when there was a knock at the door. "Susan, we can see lights, and it seems that you are dancing, we want to join the party."

Josephine and Lynn thought the DVD was a great idea, but my room was a little cramped, so they persuaded me to set up my laptop in one of the empty classrooms so that they could join in too. Quite a crowd gathered at the windows, and some of the little kids danced along with us. Our favourite routine was the kickboxing one, and I would hear the kids chanting "knee, kick, punch one, two, three" as they played in the yard. We tried an alternative routine called "the pump" a couple of times but it was less popular. For that one we had to improvise some weights. Lynn and I used tins of beans while Josephine arrived holding two huge bricks; that woman was as hard as nails. We got into the routine of "gymming", as L and J called it, at least once a week, and that seemed enough to counteract the pap. One of my favourite memories is of little Mumbiya concentrating really hard and copying all of Davina's moves until she knew them off by heart. When I returned to Namibia for a holiday over a year later, she was still chanting "knee, kick, one two three four" and kickboxing her way around the garden. Davina McCall seems like a lovely lady; I am sure she would be thrilled to know the distance her routines have travelled.

Many of the students were pretty sporty, with football and netball being favourites. During one of the school's away matches, I was asked to drive a team of girls over to Linyanti for a tournament. They were high as kites and singing all the way. My friend Cath was visiting at the time, and we had an idyllic afternoon cheering them on and providing cool drinks. We drove the winning teams home in a convoy; all the girls were standing up in the open bakkies, cheering and encouraging the drivers to race one another. I did a quick risk assessment that went off the scale, pulled over and demanded that the girls sit down. I gestured to the other drivers to slow down, but they sped off. My girls were furious to be lumbered with such a sensible killjoy.

Once a year, we had a sports day at school, which was great fun. Mr Shamwazi organised groups, and they each came up with a team name. His team was always called Frankie Fredericks after the Namibian Olympic silver medallist. Fredericks ran the 100 and 200 metres and won medals in the 1992 and 96 Olympic Games, making him the only Namibian Olympic medallist. In the London 2012 Paralympic Games, Johanna Benson won gold in the 200m. In a moving ceremony, she was presented with her medal by Frankie Fredericks himself, now a member of the International Olympic Committee. She was the Namibian flag bearer in Rio 2016, where two more athletes, Ananias Shikongo and Johannes

Nambala, brought home five medals, including a gold, between them. Athletics is well supported and taking off in Namibia. In the recent Commonwealth games in Birmingham there were bronze medals in the 100m and 200m for Shikongo and Christine Mboma. I hope Benson, Shikongo, Nambala and Mboma have become coveted team names at Simataa Senior Secondary School – surely the ultimate stamp of athletic success.

The sports day events took place on the field surrounding the schoolyard, rather ambitiously referred to as "the athletics field". It was ankle-breakingly uneven and covered in scrubby vegetation, but students had been working hard to prepare the ground in the weeks leading up to the event. They hacked away at the prickly shrubs, marked out tracks and cleared and raked some areas for field events. I was asked to supervise the long jump, which involved watching out for fouls, measuring the jumps and recording their lengths on a piece of paper. I am ashamed to say that I added a few cm to my favourite pupil's leap, who was short for her age and at quite a disadvantage. I sat at a desk under the shade of my umbrella and had a wonderful afternoon. Mr Shamwazi tooted authoritatively on his whistle, somehow persuading the young people to run as fast as they could in the searing heat. After the 200m race, two girls collapsed and because I owned a first aid kit, I was sent to revive them. I gave them a drink, put a damp cloth on their heads and let them sit out the rest of the competition under my umbrella. The toughest event was the long-distance race, which was of indeterminate length. It involved Mr Tatelo driving out into the bush with a bakkie load of students, dropping them off and then heading home as they ran barefoot back to school. He reckoned it was about 5 km but admitted that one year it had been more like ten, as he had been listening to his favourite song on the radio and got rather carried away before remembering to do the drop off.

By far the most exercise I ever got was at the weekend when I visited Katima's premier night spot, Flame. It was a dilapidated and rather grubby nightclub and the only place to dance away a Saturday night. I picked the girls up, and we would head over, usually after a sundowner or two by the river. Attitudes to drink-driving were rather relaxed, and with so few vehicles on the road at night it wasn't deemed an issue. I initially baulked at this information, but after a few dreary booze-free nights out I succumbed to local tradition and simply drove slowly. Mr Tatelo said that nothing could go wrong as long as you stayed in second gear (except maybe to the gearbox).

The dance floor at Flame was hilarious, unintentionally springy and surrounded by mirrors. Most people would stand in front of the mirrors and check out their own moves unselfconsciously. The music was fantastic – an exhilarating mix of Namibian stars such as Sunny Boy, Qonja and Gazza, and American chart artists like Beyonce and Rihanna. Kwaito music was hugely popular, born in post-apartheid Soweto; this music often carried a political, anti-apartheid message. The DJ took requests and regularly played the current favourites repeatedly. He once played Shakira seven times in a row (it reminded me of the tape I made when I was an earnest thirteen year old called *Repeat November Rain,* which had nothing but *November Rain* by Guns 'n' Roses on the entire cassette, both sides). The whole place had a rather teenage air to it: binge listening to your favourite songs while dancing with your own reflection. I think that's why I loved it so much.

Some nights we danced from 10 p.m. until three or four in the morning, and my whole body would ache the next day. Most nights a group of women lit *braais* and sold meat around the front of the club. It was delicious, if somewhat messy to eat, and went perfectly with a cool Windhoek Lager. Occasionally, there was added drama, like the time someone turned up with a gun or the night Josephine got trapped in the cesspit of a toilet and we didn't find her for ages. She had been texting SOS messages but then ran out of credit and mentally prepared to spend the night there. She was really angry when we released her, and we had to buy her lots of beers to calm her down.

Another potential form of exercise was swimming. Most of the lodges had pools and were happy to allow non-residents to have a dip for a small charge, although I later learnt that this sometimes only applied if you were white. Unfortunately, the nearest ones had tiny plunge pools, not very useful for clocking up the lengths. Occasionally Jane, Carol and I drove out to one of the more remote lodges with a decent sized pool. We once found a small mouse frantically swimming around; Jane rescued it with a large leaf before we all leapt in. I tried not to think about how much mouse wee and poo I probably ingested during that dip.

The obvious if terrifying place to go for a swim was the mighty Zambezi River. We would regularly spot hippos and crocs as we sat on the banks. Some Saturday nights, having a G&T at Hippo Lodge, I would stare out across the dark river and torture myself by imagining being forced to swim across to the other side. We had endless drunken discussions about how much money we would need to be offered before agreeing to jump in (at least a cool million – pounds, that is – not Namibian dollars). Everyone knew a friend or a friend of a friend who had been attacked by a crocodile or a hippo, and fatalities were an annual occurrence. I was once out on the river with Eddie, Kenny and Morne when our boat ran aground on a sandbank. Morne hopped out and pushed us off, and we saw an enormous croc plop into the water 100m away. I've never seen anyone move so fast, and I had horrible dreams about it for ages.

Eddie said that the only safe place to go for a swim was in the shallow, rocky rapids as no dangerous animals would be there. This area was out near the bridge to Zambia and was christened "the beach" by locals. It was a great place to hang out on a Sunday afternoon. People would turn up with *braais*, beers and stereos and laze around in the water. The only downside was that the notion of taking your litter home didn't exist, so the banks could get pretty scummy, and there was often a lot of broken glass. You might be safe from a crocodile attack, but the risk of laceration and major blood loss was very real. I always kept my sandals on as I scrambled around before plunging into the deep pools. It still freaked me out a bit, and I never fully relaxed, but it was a fun place to spend the day.

Mr Shamwazi

Long jump on sports day

CHAPTER 10
SCIENCE CLUB

The Namibian Science Fair is a long-running project aiming to develop an interest in science, maths and engineering among school students. It is an annual event sponsored by NamPower in conjunction with the National Commission on Research, Science, and Technology (NCRST). The goal was to develop critical thinking, planning and presentation skills and provide public recognition for students who worked hard. It has grown in size and success over the years and students from every region of Namibia take part.

When I took up my job in 2006, there was a drive to encourage participation from all regions, and in particular rural government schools that had not entered the competition in any number. The Department for

Education encouraged VSO to lend their support, and that year the Zambezi Region sent teams to the Science Fair for the first time and came home with a gold medal for a solar oven project. In the more densely populated Oshikoto and Ohangwena regions, volunteers were assigned posts specifically geared towards supporting teachers in developing science clubs and organising regional science fairs.

It is no mean feat to set up a science club in a school. In UK state schools and academies, teachers are rarely given additional time or money for running them. They take place at lunchtime or after school and must be squeezed into an already hectic day. Organisations such as STEM Learning (STEM stands for Science, Technology, Engineering and Maths) provide some money, resources and ideas, but nothing will happen unless a teacher takes on the additional workload. Like many great sounding initiatives, the reality is often poorly funded and involves an increased workload for already stretched teachers. In Namibia, there was the additional issue that many of the science teachers were inexperienced in standard laboratory practicals, let alone additional science club project ideas. One of my jobs would be to set up a science club at Simataa, come up with some project ideas and get some participants to the National Science Fair finals.

Like the worldwide status quo, there was an overrepresentation of privately-educated pupils at the Science Fair finals. When I last checked, there were 1,723 schools in Namibia, with a handful more under construction. 119 of these were private schools and 1,604 were government schools. Anecdotally, in 2005 over 80% of the Science Fair finalists came from private schools. So, under 7% of schools were providing 80% of the best science projects. Sound familiar? In the UK, around 7% of the population are privately educated, yet these individuals make up 71% of senior judges, 62% of senior armed forces officers, 53% of senior diplomats and 44% of the *Sunday Times Rich List*[3]. Stagnating social mobility creates unfair societies; young people develop the idea that a particular study or career route is "not for the likes of me."

I am not sure who was responsible for confronting the issue of wider participation within the Science Fairs; maybe it was the NCRST or the corporate social interest

---

[3] These statistics come from the Sutton Trust and Social Mobility Commission.

arm of NamPower. Maybe a directive came from the Department of Education or NAMCOL. Whoever it was, they did a brilliant job, and the Namibian National Science Fairs are now inclusive, inspirational events where everyone is encouraged to take part. This was not about detracting from those private school pupils' achievements but making sure that all pupils, whatever school they went to, got a chance to get involved. Perhaps the UK government could get some advice from them. I was overwhelmed by my experience of taking a group of Simataa students along to the Science Fair finals in Windhoek. It made me feel that I was doing something useful and worthwhile.

Kees, Jane and Carol had already set up a series of science clubs, and a number of the Zambezi schools were keen to take part. Mr Malapo had supervised a successful entry last year where a group of students investigated different ways of making glue by boiling down hooves. I might suggest that to our science club coordinator in Cumbria. "Investigating the comparative stickiness of glue produced from Herdwick, Swaledale and Texel sheep," has a nice ring to it. The initial science club meeting was organised by Mr Malapo, and it was very popular; we struggled to fit all the interested students into the lab. I asked the pupils to arrange themselves into small groups and share some ideas about possible projects. Sitting at my desk now, I have just Googled "science project ideas for kids" and instantly found hundreds of projects to choose from. With no electricity in Chinchimane and slow, unreliable internet in Katima, this was not an option for us. We had a couple of useful books in the Teacher's Resource Centre, but other than that we had to rely on our own ideas.

Over the next few weeks, numbers dwindled to a manageable, dedicated few, and the students chose their projects. Some worked in groups while two of the senior students worked alone. Dumisa set up an agricultural science project in the school garden, growing various vegetables under different fertiliser and irrigation schemes. Susan Meleke wanted to investigate different low-tech water purification systems. One group of younger boys explored various natural and synthetic clothes dyes and compared how well they held their colour in the sun and after washing. A final group of girls built a solar oven like last year's gold medal winners. I suggested a whole range of project ideas to the students and was really impressed that they all chose research that might improve life in rural Namibia. In addition to their own investigations, Addie was also running a regional competition where students had to create their own hot-air balloon out of paper, wire and plastic bags. The "balloons" would be inflated using a hairdryer, and the winners would be the ones that gained the most height and stayed aloft for the longest. I got in a huff because this immediately put all the schools without electricity, like mine, at a real disadvantage as we could not test our models until the day of the competition.

Science club met once a week, and students worked on their inquiries in their own time too. Dumisa got started straight away by clearing and planting out sections of the school garden. Behind the hostel buildings was a fenced-in patch of about $2,000m^2$ (half an acre to you, dad) where the students grew various fruit and vegetables as part of their agricultural studies lessons. Beatrice Siambango, one of the best teachers I have ever met, was in charge, and as a result it was incredibly productive. The big problem was pests. Cattle and goats would trample the fence to get to the lush vegetation, and birds would peck at any emerging fruit and seeds. Old mosquito nets were draped over the rows of crops, and the fence was continually being reinforced. Beatrice sold any excess produce to fund new fencing materials.

Dumisa planted rows of tomatoes and corn and fertilised some with dried manure that he had collected, some with chemical fertiliser from the hardware store in town and some were left with no additional nutrients at all. In an ideal world, organic fertiliser would provide food security. Our world is far from ideal, and without chemical fertiliser, the soil becomes mineral deficient, and yields are reduced. The minerals replaced by the addition of manure are not always enough to sustain year on year growth, and the soil degrades over time. I was reading about this in the *Guardian* recently, and according to Professor Ken Giller, a soil scientist at Wageningen University in the Netherlands, "One cow can produce about 15kg of nitrogen in manure annually, but a healthy maize crop needs up to 100kg of nitrogen a hectare."

On average, farmers in Africa harvest about one tonne of maize per hectare, whereas their American counterparts reap up to 12 tonnes. In addition, according to this article, some economists claim international fertiliser companies are manipulating the market by charging certain African nations more than richer countries. My own experience to support this is that I sat next to a fertiliser salesman at a wedding once; he developed the African market for his company. He was wealthy (or so he said) and seemed slippery and lacking in morals to me because he tried to chat me up while already having a girlfriend. Dumisa's research supported current knowledge, and his chemically enriched soil produced a much greater yield. I suggested he share his findings with the agricultural college and see whether they could advise him on the next step.

On the sandy track as you drove into Chinchimane there was a cluster of buildings associated with the agricultural college in Katima Mulilo. Similar structures could be found in many of the larger villages. They acted as farming cooperatives where mechanical equipment such as tractors could be hired, and training was given on how to use them, although I only saw one tractor during my entire time living in Chinchimane.

Research was carried out at several institutions. I have since learnt they were investigating the effectiveness of growing leguminous plants to replenish nitrate levels in the soil. Legumes such as peas and beans have evolved a symbiotic relationship with nitrogen-fixing bacteria found in root nodules. These bacteria use an enzyme called nitrogenase to convert inert atmospheric nitrogen into ammonia. It has long been understood that planting legumes and ploughing the vegetation back into the ground is an effective way of restoring nitrate levels. The college wanted to see if they would grow effectively in the Namibian climate. If Dumisa had extended his project further to include this, I think it would have been a medal winner. As it was, I left him to his own devices a little too much, and it seems his time at the agricultural college was spent flirting with the pretty secretary and eating experimental tomatoes.

The group of boys had great fun cutting a roll of pale fabric into miniature T-shirt shapes and dying each one. They made various dyes from fruit, berries and crushed flowers, following instructions handed down from their grans. I bought them packets of synthetic dye from town. They hung the mini clothes out in the sun and compared rates of fading over the coming weeks. The tiny, fluttering washing lines looked surreal. I thought it was a great project, and the lads were incredibly well organised. The young girls were less prepared, and their solar oven seemed to consist of a piece of cardboard covered in silver foil. They cracked an egg onto it to see if it would cook, but Jude bounded over and scoffed it.

Susan was a solemn, bright student who had aspirations to become a nurse. She made a sediment water filter following instructions from a science textbook. Inside a plastic container, she layered charcoal, fine sand, coarse sand and gravel; a piece of muslin cloth at the bottom completed it. The filter was designed to remove unwanted particulate matter from the water, leaving it safe to drink. Susan was extending the project to see how effective UV light was at killing any remaining pathogens in the water; she had read that exposure to six hours of sunlight was enough to kill bacteria such as salmonella and E. coli. We did not have the equipment to test for bacteria, so I suggested that we get in touch with Nam Water (Namibian Water Corporation Ltd). As was often the case, someone at school was related to someone who worked for Nam Water, and he agreed to meet Susan and me, talk to us about measuring bacterial load in water and give us a tour of the Zambezi water purification plant.

I picked Susan up one Saturday and we headed over to the site. The area along the banks of the Zambezi had changed dramatically in the previous twelve months with the development of the Zambezi Waterfront Project. This state-funded venture aimed to build a tourist park and facilities to rival those downriver in Zambia and Zimbabwe. Initial groundworks had begun, and large embankments of sand and earth were constructed to act as foundations. The area was supposed to be out of bounds to the public, but everyone ignored this, and the banks became a popular spot for an evening stroll.

The week before, a huge JCB backhoe loader (I have two small children, I know diggers) had been working there when it overbalanced, teetered on the edge of the bank and slowly upended itself into the river. It caused great excitement and much hilarity, and half the town flocked to see it. As Susan and I drove past, we could see its incongruous yellow form protruding from the water. The flimsy piece of regulatory tape around it was being ignored, and kids were swarming all over it; Katima finally had a play park. Ten years later, in March 2016, the Zambezi Waterfront was temporarily closed down amid allegations of deceit and dishonest administration; it seems it still hasn't quite got going. Half a mile downstream from the backhoe loader was the NamWater purification plant.

A gentleman called Dessie showed us around and talked to Susan at length about how to test water for bacteria. I confess I switched off and spent my time gazing across the river to Zambia, daydreaming and hoping to spot a hippo. Dessie asked whether we would like to climb up inside the water tower where water is pumped, and levels are recorded. Susan agreed straight away, but I was a little more reluctant. The water tower was a concrete cylinder rising about 10m above the river's surface and entered through a small hobbit door on the bank. Once inside, a series of metal ladders and platforms took us right up to the top, where a circle of sky was visible. It was cold and gloomy inside and as expected, smelled pretty dank. Dessie let us go first, and once Susan and I were inside, I heard the heavy door clang shut behind us. Shit! As our eyes adjusted to the gloom, I panicked. Had Dessie locked us in? Was he going to keep us as sex slaves inside the water tower? Would anyone hear us screaming this far from the town? Maybe we could hold our breath and swim to freedom through one of the outflow pipes. Could Susan even swim? I would have to swim for it and come back to rescue her …

Just as I was about to kick off my shoes and jump in, the door opened again, and Dessie's beaming faced appeared lit by a huge torch. "Sorry ladies, I forgot the light. Right, let's go up a see the view from the top of the tower." My heart was pounding, and I still didn't quite trust him, so I kept my wits about me on the clamber up, poised for flight or fight. I couldn't fully appreciate the panorama from the top platform. Once safely out and on the riverbank, Susan posed for some photographs and collected a water testing kit; I felt emotionally drained.

Science Fair heats were held in the different school circuits. The Chinchimane one would be here at Simataa School. The students had to prepare presentation posters explaining their research, and they would be questioned by the judges, Addie and Mr Mwilima. I bought sheets of sugar paper, glue and a packet of marker pens from the stationery shop in town, along with an expensive colour ink cartridge for printing photographs. The students worked hard to present their findings, and the clothes dye poster in particular was wonderfully colourful and eye-catching.

On the day of the heats, Addie arrived early in the morning to help set up. We arranged tables in one of the empty classrooms, and I double-checked the catering arrangements. With some of the NamPower funding, we could provide lunch for all the entrants, and the kitchen staff were preparing chicken, pap and cool cans of *Fanta* for everyone to share. We had primary, junior and senior entries from Chinchimane School, Kanono and Linyanti and overall, there were eighteen projects to judge. There was a lovely, excited atmosphere around school, and Mrs Mahoto made a rousing speech. I was proud of everyone's hard work and was thrilled when Dumisa, Susan and the dye boys all got through. The regional heats would be held at the teacher training college in Katima in a month's time, and if they were successful there, the projects would be taken to Windhoek for the national finals.

We spent the month between the circuit and regional competitions tweaking the posters and carrying out extension projects. I had arranged for a bakkie to take us all to Katima, and the students sang the whole way. Thankfully, this time the driver was sober and the brakes intact. NAMCOL had provided engineering displays, puzzles and activities for the students, and in between judging, they wandered around the exhibition. I had been asked to judge this time and was given eight projects to score, not including any from my own school. The judging criteria were strict, and I found it difficult to be objective when I could see how much effort the young people had put into their work. There were some great solar-powered toy cars and an interesting irrigation system based on collecting dew on large plastic sheets. At the end of a long day, the twelve successful projects were announced, and I felt like crying when all three from Simataa were chosen. We stopped off at the OK Superstore so I could buy everyone a fizzy drink and celebratory sweets before we returned victorious to Chinchimane just as the sun was setting. We now had two months to organise our trip to Windhoek.

The intervening months flew by. Addie had organised a bus to take the students down to Windhoek; I was in Swakopmund catching up with an old friend, so I had arranged to meet them at their hostel. The students were high as kites when I arrived. Only two had been to Windhoek before, and few had spent time away from their families. I was sent off to the supermarket straight away to buy sandwiches, drinks and snacks for everyone, and then we prepared a rota for the staff to supervise and organise activities. I had been given £200 by my Godparents and used it to take the group out for a treat; after a vote, the unanimous winner was a trip to Maerua Mall followed by burgers and the cinema. I was a bit disappointed; I had really wanted to take them on a safari trip to the Daan Viljoen nature reserve, but the group had shown a fairly typical disinterest in looking at wildlife. Josephine's take on this was, "If we want to look at animals, we can watch the cows and goats. They at least give something back, better than any good-for-nothing leopard or lion that just wants to eat me."

We gave them free time to look around the mall. A few had brought spending money, but most just window shopped. The younger ones lacked confidence and stuck together in a giggling, near-hysterical flock. Some took this time to meet up with family members; many of the brightest, most ambitious young people moved to Windhoek to seek their fortune, and those who found success would send money home to their relations in the north. Every person with a decent job was supporting another twenty back in the village. One lucky boy was treated to a fashionable new outfit by an older brother employed by a city engineering firm. The others looked on enviously as he strutted around with his baseball cap on back to front and his trousers hanging around his bottom. I thought everyone in the group looked great; they had all dug out their best or borrowed outfits for the occasion.

The students started to gather at our pre-arranged time outside the modern five-screen cinema, I was impressed that everyone was on time despite not a single watch between them. Most of the students had watched some TV at their town homes in Katima, but none had visited a cinema before and there was much excitement as the show time drew near. I bought everyone a drink and some popcorn, and we traipsed into the cinema to find our seats and settled down to watch *Transformers*. It was incredibly loud, and even for me, starved of the big screen for nearly two years, it was overwhelming. During a violent, noisy fight between Optimus Prime and Megatron, I noticed two young boys in front of me clutching each other. I leaned forward and was horrified to see them shaking and sobbing, presumably terrified. I asked them if they would like to come outside with me, but they insisted on sitting it out. When I spoke to the pair afterwards, they maintained they had really enjoyed it and asked if they could watch it again. I wished I had insisted on the nature ramble.

No one showed lasting signs of distress and there were no nightmares so, bright and early the following morning, we headed over to the Windhoek Private School where the National Science Fair finals were held. The school hall was filled with display boards and trestle tables, and each group had been allocated a spot. Susan and Dumisa got set up straight away, and I helped the lads set up their dye project; they had brought a mini washing line with some of their samples, and the whole thing looked fab. Accompanying teachers were asked to help with the judging, and when everyone was set up, we were given some training on what to look for. Our job was to draw up a shortlist from which external judges would allocate bronze, silver, and gold medals. I loved walking around that hall reading about the research that the young people had done, made all the more impressive by the limited resources so many had to hand.

One of the joys of being a teacher is seeing burgeoning talent and realising that tipping point when their ingenuity and imagination have exceeded your own; they aren't learning from you anymore but have taken the skills you taught them and are heading off on their own. After drawing up individual shortlists, there was an opportunity for discussion before the potential medal winners were presented to the main judges. I got into a disagreement about a senior project done by a teenaged white girl on her family's game farm. From what I could gather, she had stood at the end of their driveway for a few hours at a time and counted the traffic. She had produced a bar chart of different forms of transport to show the proportions of cars, bakkies, combis, trucks and buses and concluded that there were too many bakkies on the road. Her poster was beautifully presented with glossy photographs and typed, printed text (all of ours were handwritten). A number of other teachers had rated her project highly, and it was poised to make the shortlist. I argued that it contained little science, was a thin piece of work, and contained only simple observation. I suggested (perhaps unwisely) that people had been swayed by the impressive presentation and that this was a mark for style over substance. I wonder, was I prejudiced against her? She had certainly put effort into the project but was from a wealthy family and had computers, printers, and display materials at her disposal. Others had produced so much more in-depth research with so little.

I lost the argument, and her project went through. Dumisa and Susan had made the shortlist, but I was sad to hear that the lads had not. The feedback said they could not answer questions about their project very well. Perhaps they were too shy, or maybe I had helped them too much, and they had been rather muddled in their understanding. They did not seem to mind, fuelled on sweets and content with their Science Fair goody bag filled with stickers, pens and other much-coveted items.

We then had the customary wait of a few hours as the judges made their decisions. These things would take an age back home, but here such formalities could really stretch my patience. We sat around and chatted, and the students took the opportunity to have a look at the other work on display. We were directed back into the hall at around teatime and took seats on gym benches and plastic chairs arranged at the end of the room. The head judge gave an inspiring speech about being Namibia's proud future, and everyone sang the national anthem. As ever, this got me rather emotional, and I could feel tears welling. The judge started reading out bronze medal winners, and when he read out Susan Meleke's name, some tears spilt over. She walked proudly to the front to receive her prize, and when she returned to her seat, all the Zambezi Region students cheered, and I gave her a hug; we held sweaty hands for the rest of the ceremony. Susan was the only medal winner from Simataa School, but the Zambezi Region as a whole went home with six.

We had one more day in Windhoek and planned to drive the group 10km out of the city to visit Heroes' Acre, a war memorial built in 2002 to "foster a spirit of patriotism and nationalism, and to pass on the legacy to the future generations of Namibia." I wasn't entirely sure about fostering a spirit of nationalism, but I was keen to visit the site to pay my respects and learn more about

Namibia's recent conflict. The South West Africa People's Organisation (SWAPO) battled for twenty-three long years against South African occupation and rule. My colleagues and friends had grown up under the apartheid regime, and South Africa Defence Force (SADF) soldiers had been stationed in the bush around their village homes. Mr Chalo told me of a bunch of soldiers who would play football with the village kids when he was growing up; they gave them sweets and let them wear their hats. He said all the boys wanted to be known as "Steve" like their favourite soldier, although when their mothers heard them calling each other Steve, they would get a clout around the ear. This rather sweet story belies a bitter, violent war that claimed thousands of lives.

There are tales of battles where SADF used helicopters and grenades against Namibians on the ground armed with a few AK47s and bows and arrows. But the Namibians did not surrender; legendary leaders such as Kaxumba KaNdola spoke rousing words to their comrades: "Victory is ours; the land will be free; there shall be peace again and respect for human dignity." And he was right. Since Independence Day on March 21st, 1990, Namibia's elected president has been one of the heroes of the struggle either as soldier, leader or political activist. First Sam Nujoma, then Hifikepunye Pohamba, who was in power during my time in Namibia, and most recently Hage Geingob who assumed office in 2015. Despite some unrest amongst young voters, it is difficult to envisage a party other than SWAPO leading Namibia while the fight for independence is in living memory.

I was moved by Heroes' Acre; I cannot imagine a decent soul who would not be. Thousands tortured, killed and dumped in mass graves are commemorated here. The shrine is dominated by a 34m high obelisk rising from the centre of stepped tiers and platforms. A stunning bronze mural spanned the base, illustrating a timeline of oppression and struggle. Viewed from left to right, it began by depicting Germany's colonial rule from 1884 to 1914, followed by apartheid and the 1960 petitioning of the UN for independence. The final scenes portrayed victory and the declaration of independence with the new flag flying high. The entire site was huge, spanning 2.96km^2, including parade grounds and a grandstand for 5,000 people. That might not sound big, but it is enough to seat 0.2% of the Namibian population. Wembley Stadium would need to double its 90,000 capacity to match that. Around the site are 174 gravesites, not all of which are currently occupied.

At the inauguration event in 2002, nine national heroes and heroines had tombstones erected to honour their bravery and revolutionary spirit. Some names were well-known: Hosea Kutako, leader of the Herero people and founder member of Namibia's first Nationalist party, and Henrik Witbooi, chief of the Ikhowesin whose face appears on the N$50, N$100 and N$200 notes. I like his Nama name: !Nanseb gaib I Gâbemab, the captain who disappears in the grass. Every town of any size had a Henrik Witbooi Street and a Hosea Kutako Drive. One woman was recognised at the Heroes' Acre tombstones. Her name was Anna Kakurukaze Mungunda, and she was shot dead after setting fire to the car belonging to the mayor or police superintendent of the Old Location in Windhoek. The story I read said that her only son had been killed by South African forces during the Old Location uprising, an event that claimed the lives of twelve peaceful protestors. She was twenty-seven years old.

An 8m-high bronze statue commemorated those heroes whose names were not recorded. The "Unknown Soldier" held an AK-47 assault rifle in his left hand and an anti-tank grenade in his right. At his feet was a cast of Sam Nujoma's own handwriting in gold plate: "Glory to the fallen Heroes and Heroines of the motherland Namibia!" The soldier bore a striking resemblance to Sam Nujoma himself and was controversially designed and made by the Mansudae Art Studio in Pyongyang, North Korea.

The students were respectful and sombre throughout the trip, but some light relief was delivered when we bought refreshments in the café, and a bold chacma baboon tried to steal Dumisa's Cornetto. I bought a copy of Sam Nujoma's autobiography, *Where Others Wavered,* and started to read it on the drive home. It is a hefty 465 pages long and rather impenetrable in places. I am ashamed to say I still haven't finished it. We had a heroes' welcome of our own when we finally returned to Chinchimane, and an assembly was held to celebrate the young scientists' achievements.

Working on an experiment in the laboratory

The school garden

CHAPTER 11

TRADITIONAL HEALERS

Early one morning, I arrived in the staff room to a heated discussion. Mr Shamwazi explained that hippo footprints had been spotted in the village, and everyone wondered where they had come from. Chinchimane is a long way from any water, the closest being the Linyanti River, about 30km away. In the past, this has filtered through swamps to the ephemeral Lake Liambezi. Hippos grazed channels in the wetlands, and one environmentalist's theory is that over the past 50 years, poaching has caused a decline in hippo numbers leading to the waterways growing over. Now Lake Liambezi is pretty much a dust bowl, only rarely filling with water in times of flood.

Mr Malapo reckoned a hippo must have survived for years in the fringes of the swamp and had travelled over land to Chinchimane, maybe looking for a mate. It was probably very sick and possibly dangerous. Some students had followed the footprints but lost them in dense bush. What a thrilling start to a Monday morning! We were discussing how long a hippo could survive without water, and Mr Chalo had sent a boy to the library for an encyclopedia. He was looking up "hippo" when Mr Tatelo said it was "most likely to be a man who has been witched and turned into a hippo." I snorted at the joke but then noticed that others were nodding in agreement, and Mr Chalo had abandoned his research.

"You don't really believe that do you?"

"We do; it is our culture to believe in such magic."

I looked to Lynn for clarification, and she looked a bit sheepish and shrugged. "It is true, Sue. We believe."

She explained that traditional medicine and witchcraft were part of their social fabric. Many well-educated, cosmopolitan Namibians believed in the powers of the witch doctor and traditional healer. She said that some professional people might be embarrassed and not admit to seeking advice from witch doctors or "*naka*", but they still did. If someone had done wrong or was being cursed by another, they could be turned into animals. I was surprised that a bunch of teachers could believe this, but then I'm certain that UK staff rooms are home to earnest discussions about homoeopathy and whacky conspiracy theories. Cultures around the world have belief systems that others will find dubious. The mystery of the hippo footprints was solved when a single hippo foot was found tied to a stick. Mr Simataa said some kids must have found a hippo foot (where? How?) and made the prints to trick people. Or maybe the local *naka* did it to advance his credentials.

That evening I asked Josephine whether she had ever used a traditional healer, and she said yes, many times, both for her and her children. If you were ill, then the first stop was always the traditional healer. Conventional medicine was only ever the second option. Treatments were mostly based on various plant roots, leaves and bark, ground up to make powders. These powders were then ingested or rubbed into small cuts made on the body. I had seen many people, particularly women, with small scars on their chest or face, usually in two or three small straight lines. Josephine said that in the case of young women these were most commonly the result of charms designed to attract men or keep hold of the man they were currently dating and get him to marry them. Such love potions were common and usually rubbed into cuts near the armpit, inner thigh or forehead close to the hairline. I thought back to my cut hair that disappeared from the rubbish pit. Had it been powdered and rubbed into the thigh of a young woman to attract the man of her dreams? If so, I hoped it had worked. Josephine said that she had bought expensive powders imported from Nigeria that could tell whether your husband was cheating on you. You dissolved the powders in his bathwater, and if he was cheating, he would turn into a snake. It sounded like a win-win situation for powder sellers and cheating men.

The use of herbs as remedies is of course common, and many medicines are based on plants. All cultures have a history of visiting wise experts for advice on illnesses, and information on successful cures is passed down the generations. The aspect of traditional healing that I found worrying was its link to witchcraft. In some African countries such as Nigeria and Tanzania, there are strongly held beliefs in witches and warlocks and associated violence against people accused of administering curses. Even young children can be accused of so-called black magic, and there have been horrific stories reported in the press of exorcisms and even murders based around such practice. Incidents like these were extremely rare in Namibia, but they did occur. In 2009 a shocking story came out of Tanzania, where people with albinism had been murdered and their bones used for witchcraft.

Albinism is a hereditary condition resulting in a complete lack of protective melanin in the skin. It is most common in sub-Saharan Africa, with an estimated one in 3,000 Namibians affected. People with albinism are visually impaired and at high risk of developing skin cancer. In addition, they are frequently stigmatised. One of the Katima volunteers was doing a lot of work with young people with albinism, aimed at providing sunscreen, sunhats, and glasses and educating friends and family about how the condition was not a curse. Stigma and discrimination still occur, but the situation is much improved, and people affected by albinism are slowly finding acceptance. Interestingly, the Herero people of Namibia see albinism as a gift from God. In 2008, the Day of Albinism was established, celebrated each year on 21st October. Namibia has shown itself a step ahead of some of its neighbours here.

Most people seemed to believe that everyone should die from old age and that if anyone died young, it was the result of a curse or evil spirit. Bad luck or misfortune could be put down to spells being cast by your enemies, and the only way to counteract this was a visit to the healer. In school, students who excelled in exams were sometimes accused of cursing the other pupils to get ahead. Mrs Mahoto told me she was regularly contacted by parents worried that their child had been cursed by another, resulting in their poor performance at school. She said that such talk caused hysteria, and the only way to quash it was by education and prayer. Lynn said that most of these accusations were fuelled by jealousy and as more and more Namibians were attaining qualifications, getting good jobs and acquiring possessions, suspicions arose that this had occurred through magical means.

I spoke to some of my students about it and asked whether they believed in curses, charms and witchcraft. Most of them said yes, and every one of them had been taken to a traditional healer at some time. Many were devoted Christians, and they were more reluctant to accept such allegations. They were taught by their preachers that the Bible forbids the practice of magic and that only God can protect them from harm. Some witch doctors said that God had the power to stop curses and charms from working, which seemed like a neat little get-out clause.

I was intrigued by the traditional healer's role in everyday life and how it contradicted the very visible religious faith. So, when Rachel and Mr Simataa invited me to a mass baptism taking place in the village one weekend, I was keen to attend. A number of local congregations were gathering, and over two hundred people were expected to attend. Such events previously took place on the Zambezi River banks, with converts being fully submerged in the water to celebrate being born again. Rather ironically, two had been killed by crocodiles, so future baptisms were moved onto dry land.

This one was taking place in the gardens of Mr Mutela's guest house. They had partly filled his swimming pool, which must have been an epic task, and were enthusiastically dunking people when we arrived. It was, as ever, incredibly hot, and I struggled to find a patch of shade. The cool water in the pool looked so inviting that I briefly considered a conversion myself. One at a time, individuals walked up to the front, and the pastor would place both hands onto their head and then lead them into the water. Prayers were said, jubilant songs were sung, and when they emerged from the water, baptised and born again, everyone cheered and ululated. To my surprise, I found the whole event incredibly emotional. To witness such joy and devotion was overwhelming. People were crying and hugging, and I felt like a fraud as I wanted to cry too.

One of the last people to be baptised was a frail old man who needed help to get into and out of the pool. Mr Simataa said that he used to be a witch doctor, but he had found the Lord and wanted to renounce all of his old ways. He wore jeans and a T-shirt but handed his traditional attire over to the preacher. This comprised a skirt and headdress made of threaded bamboo. The old man carried a staff, a knife and a tin box which contained the accoutrements of his trade. All the items were given to the priest, who held them aloft and spoke loudly. Mr Simataa translated for me. He announced the destruction of his evil trade, the contents of the tin were to be buried, and the old man would start a new life with Jesus. After the baptism, I wanted to have a look inside the box and managed to sidle over to the preacher. He said the objects inside were dangerous and he would not usually let people handle them, but because I was a privileged visitor to Namibia I could see them. The box looked like an old tea caddy and contained bundles of dried twigs and leaves, some animal fur and bones and an odd-looking gnarled stump which the priest explained was the hood from a cobra. No sign of my hair.

I couldn't imagine the importance that some people placed on this strange collection of objects, in the same way that I find religious paraphernalia incomprehensible. Mr Simataa told me that they had great commercial value, and it was most likely that after the ceremonial burying, they would be dug up again and sold. I asked him how someone became a witch doctor, and he told me it was believed by some to be a calling. Ancestors bestowed talents on an individual, and they were put through a series of tests to prove their worth. He said that some could become ill for many years as they developed their powers. I joked that we should follow the priest to see where they buried the box so we could dig it up and get rich. No one laughed.

Visiting a traditional healer could be expensive, and prices varied enormously. Imenda told me that when things weren't working out between her and her child's father, she visited a witch doctor with her mum. They were charged a N$500 deposit (about £50), and after seeing the required results (her boyfriend moving back in), they would have to pay a further N$4,000 – equivalent to a teacher's monthly salary. Apparently, this type of no win, no fee set up was common, and things could get nasty if customers didn't pay up. In the end, Imenda said that she threw away all the charms she had bought and refused to spend any more money on them. She believed in true love, and if a man had to be charmed to stay with her and their baby, then he really wasn't the man they needed. The witch doctor told her that there would be serious consequences, but she said that she would put her faith in God to protect her. I couldn't help feeling that she had exchanged one mystical belief system for another, and she would do better to take her future into her own hands and out of the clouds, but at least praying was free. Ten years down the line, she's a fantastic single, working mum to a gorgeous, bright little boy, and I think she and her own mum can take full credit for that.

I heard stories about people visiting witch doctors before job interviews to improve their chances of success. Those who were appointed were duly accused of cursing their rivals. It all sounded rather emotionally exhausting and expensive, and I wondered how much it impacted daily life. Lynn said that for most educated people of our generation, witch doctor consultations were reserved for matters of health and love. Apparently, at one point, it was suggested by the health minister that some traditional healers should be certified, as they achieved positive results when treating particular ailments. It was a short debate that went silent, much like Prince Charles and his wittering about homoeopathy and the NHS. I suspect that Namibian politicians approach the topic of traditional healers in the same way that ours approach religion: they can't speak out if they think it's all rubbish for fear of alienating a huge chunk of the electorate, so instead just quietly imply they are believers while getting on with the job of running the country.

Of course, the big issue with visiting the witch doctor before the medical doctor was that demonstrably successful treatment would be delayed. In a country where geography and economics meant delays for most people anyway, this could prove fatal. I got some insight into the impact of this from Lynn's boyfriend, an interesting character called Dr Vanegas. Guillermo Vanegas was from Ecuador; he was well-travelled, charming and an expert on the treatment of HIV. He was much older than Lynn and had wooed her with a winning combination of enthusiastic salsa dancing and rude jokes. They made a brilliant couple, and I really enjoyed spending time with them. Guillermo researched the effect that traditional healers and their treatments were having on the fight against HIV and AIDS. It wasn't just the delay in starting antiretroviral therapy (ART), but some sexual practises advocated by witch doctors increased the likelihood of virus transmission.

He worked with a group of people receiving highly active antiretroviral therapy (HAART) and HIV-positive pregnant women who were part of the prevention of mother-to-child transmission programme (PMTCT). He carried out detailed surveys about their sexual knowledge and practises and collated it alongside other medical colleagues into a report with the catchy title of: *Quantitative Study to Assess Sexual Behaviour Amongst HAART/PMTCT Clients in the Caprivi Region*. He gave me a copy; it was pretty explicit and full of racy diagrams. Josephine waved a page in my face entitled *Cycle of Male and Female Sexual Response,* which displayed an erect penis complete with small dashes to indicate movement and an arty splash of semen alongside a vagina with a massively swollen clitoris.

"This is why she is with him. This! This here!" she said, whacking the page for effect and hitting me about the head with it.

When the pair of them had stopped cackling, I settled down to read the report properly, although they insisted on reading it over my shoulder and regularly supplying their opinion. Two hundred HIV-positive patients were interviewed confidentially and asked whether they had ever used *muti* during sex. *Muti* is the collective word for any traditional medicine, but particularly one used to increase sexual arousal or performance (also known as *mulyane* in the Silozi language and *musamu* in Subia). Men would usually ingest powders to increase the size of their penis or to make their erection last longer (described rather competitively as "being able to last more rounds"). 83% of men questioned admitted to using *muti*. Usually, this was taken in a drink but occasionally rubbed onto the penis (ouch!). I don't know whether this botanical Viagra actually did anything. Maybe it had a confidence-boosting placebo effect, maybe it did bugger all. 68% of the women questioned couldn't tell whether their partner had taken it or not.

The truth was that so many men took it all the time, no one had a *muti*-free experience for comparison. The frightening statistic was that none of the men and women used a condom all the time before they knew their HIV status, and well over half of those questioned never used a condom at all. There was no question in the survey about whether condom use changed after they knew they were carrying the virus – a significant omission. These figures have undoubtedly improved in the years since 2005, when the report was published.

Muti for women was a more ominous affair. In the majority of cases, it was applied to the vagina as well as being ingested. Josephine showed me a packet; it looked like fine tea leaves with a little extra grit and bark. She grinned and said I should have a go. "Rub it in your pussy; it will make it nice and tight," she said, clenching her fist for extra emphasis. I politely declined and asked why on earth women would want to do such a thing. Apparently, local custom dictates that women should not produce normal vaginal lubrication; such ladies are known as "watery women." Any physical sign that a woman was ready for sex and enjoying sex was actively discouraged. The powders would make the vagina dry, tight, hot and presumably sore. Trying to imitate a vagina being taken by force seemed to be the historical sexual norm.

I asked my friends if they had ever used it. They had when they were younger, but less now and they much preferred sex without it. The idea that women could show they enjoyed sex had gained momentum, particularly in urban areas. Apart from the pain, the negative side effect of applying *muti* was the increased risk of abrasions and lacerations, making the likelihood of HIV transmission much greater. This was surely one of the contributing factors to Namibia's AIDS statistics. I asked whether female genital mutilation (FGM) was practised in Namibia, something that regularly makes the press; FGM awareness has been introduced to the citizenship curriculum in the UK. Thankfully this was not practised in any of the regions in Namibia, although Joso said sometimes the Oshiwambo people might cut the labia or perineum as a form of healing for some ailments. Quite what could be cured by making a cut between the front bottom and back, I have no idea. Apparently, this is discouraged now because of AIDS.

One interesting statistic in Guillermo's report was about people's knowledge and experience of anal and oral sex. Apparently, more people were familiar with anal sex than oral, a figure that I'm pretty sure would be reversed in Europe, although maybe the tsunami of internet porn has changed that. The ladies and I swapped tales of experiences and techniques in some raucous beer-fuelled conversations; I wonder whether this is what VSO had in mind when they composed their slogan, "Sharing skills, changing lives"?

Traditional Zambezi dress

CHAPTER 12
GLOBAL EDUCATION

Every year, VSO encouraged groups of volunteers to arrange Global Education Conferences. The rather grand title for these gatherings belied their most important function; a chance for us to socialise, explore different parts of the country and learn about each other's work alongside interesting local traditions and issues. They were organised completely by volunteers with a small VSO budget provided for food, transport and accommodation. It was a huge treat, and I felt guilty setting off for my first conference, knowing I was getting to see and learn about parts of Namibia that my new colleagues and friends in Chinchimane may never get the chance to visit. The first one took place a couple of months after I arrived, and its focus was conservation.

The conference was based around the magnificent Etosha National Park. If you ever get the chance to visit Namibia, you must go to Etosha; it is incredible. Planning was done through a series of emails, text messages, and word of mouth; we arranged to meet at the Cheetah Conservation Fund in Otjiwarongo. We had a night's accommodation booked there in shared safari tents. I bagsied one with Rachael, Patricia, Vik and Debs, who I hadn't seen for ages. As much as I was eager to learn about Namibian wildlife, I was more interested in catching up with the girls.

The centre was aimed at educating people, particularly farmers, about cheetah conservation. Namibia is home to an estimated 3,500 adult cheetahs, about 35% of the still-dwindling global population. It was a relaxing spot on a panoramic high plateau surrounded by grassland. They had a number of captive cheetahs, rescued as orphaned cubs or from traps, which could not be released back into the wild. Cheetahs are endangered, and their main threats are habitat loss and conflict with farmers. I picked up some interesting cheetah-related information between bottles of Savannah Dry cider and catching up on gossip. Cheetahs are outcompeted by lions, leopards, and even hyena. These larger animals will steal their prey and kill them, and as a result, cheetahs avoid overlapping ranges. In national parks and nature conservancies, the top predators can thrive, driving the cheetahs away. Approximately 90% of cheetahs live outside protected areas on private farmland where they will inevitably face battles with farmers over livestock.

An enthusiastic, middle-aged lady called Jenny showed us around the centre; she had armpit hairs poking out of her Iron Maiden T-shirt, and long, sun-bleached greying hair, and I thought she was super cool. Jenny explained some of the methods they were trialling to help cheetahs and farmers live alongside one another. They breed and train giant Anatolian Shepherd Dogs, which are then adopted by local farmers to put amongst their livestock herds– usually goats but also sheep and cattle. These enormous dogs are placed with the herd as young puppies and grow up with an instinct to protect them. The programme has had some success with over five hundred dogs placed with farmers and a waiting list for puppies.

Another interesting method was to place a female donkey and her foal in with a calving herd. Donkeys are fierce protectors of their young and are aggressive to intruders. They will chase away dogs, jackals and cheetahs. Reported livestock losses are down to zero in some areas, and with the introduction of a new "cheetah-friendly" meat-labelling system, consumers can make informed choices about the meat they buy, although most of the meat I saw for sale around Katima was hanging from a tree without a label in sight. They produced heaps of advice for farmers on reducing livestock losses without resorting to killing the predators, like corralling them at night and avoiding areas with trees – the perfect cheetah vantage point. It all made perfect sense, although if my livelihood and my family's survival depended on my herd of cattle, I suppose I might not be so enthusiastic about local wildlife. Their efforts seem to be working, though; local farmers are taking their advice on board, and cheetah numbers in Namibia have at least stopped declining for the time being. I was rather envious of Jenny; she clearly loved her job, and it had a really positive impact.

After a night at the conservation centre, we were all going to head north to Etosha National Park to go wildlife watching and meet some of the rangers. I was very excited; in another life, I think I would like to be a wildlife ranger. Some folk were going to buy provisions en route while others were going to clear up the camp at the cheetah sanctuary. Patricia, Rachael, and I agreed to be the reconnaissance party. We would set off first to reserve a large camp spot at Okaukuejo camp near Etosha's south gate. There are few tarred roads in Namibia. If you look at a map, there is basically one main road running north to south with small roads, mostly untarred, branching off here and there and a busier network around the large towns. We set off from the conservation camp in Patricia's Volvo estate car, stereo on loud (ABBA and Elton John, as I recall) singing along loudly and badly, sleep deprived, gently hungover and giddy with excitement about our weekend away. The journey was supposed to take about two hours.

We had set off after breakfast to arrive well in time for lunch. The landscape in this area was rather monotonous, featureless dense shrub, and we drove along the straight road for ages, cheerfully singing. After about an hour, Rachael piped up that she thought we should have seen some road signs at that point. We drove on a bit further, then saw a sign for a place called Otavi, which none of us had heard of before. I got that gnawing, worried feeling in my tummy, the dawning realisation that something has gone a bit wrong. Patricia had a map buried deep in the boot, so we stopped for a rummage and inevitably confirmed that we were not heading in the right direction. Somehow, given only two roads to choose from in the entire area, we had chosen the wrong one and driven miles off course. I have a frighteningly poor sense of direction and in company will always assume that someone else knows the way. It seems we all fell into that same category.

We were now deep in game farm country, miles from anywhere, miles from Etosha and hopelessly late for our assigned task. We decided that the best plan was to cut across country and loop back towards Etosha at Outjo. To slow us down further, the road had gates positioned across it every few miles, presumably to control the movement of animals. We fully expected to encounter a locked one, probably right at the end, but agreed we'd just ram it if necessary, possibly holding hands like Thelma and Louise. Thankfully they were all unlocked because, as we know, that story did not end well. We finally arrived mid-afternoon, hungry, irritable and thoroughly sick of ABBA and Elton John. Everyone was camped up and made endless fun of us for being such befuddled idiots.

Late that afternoon, we drove around Etosha to visit some of the watering holes and look for wildlife. It was a real live David Attenborough documentary, and I was blown away by the number of different animals that we saw, just cruising by doing their own thing. They were not completely oblivious to our presence, but also not troubled by it. Giraffes strode past on the skyline looking like prehistoric creatures, elephants were everywhere, and we saw a pride of lions snoozing in the last of the day's sun. That night, after a delicious *braai* of kudu steaks, we walked over to one of the watering holes near our camp and settled down with some beers to watch the animals come for an evening drink. A rhino mother and calf appeared in the gloom, and I got an immature fit of the giggles when someone farted, possibly a rhino, but most likely an over-excited wildlife spotter.

I was so completely overjoyed by the sight of all of these beautiful animals roaming free that I didn't really want to meet our guest speaker the following morning, a hunting guide called Steegh Storbeck. Steegh was paid to track animals for rich punters so that they could kill them. He talked about how hunting brought huge revenue to a poor country and how it was rigorously controlled to promote sustainability. Animals could only be hunted in particular managed areas, and strict quotas were applied.

Foreigners would pay huge sums for a licence to kill lions, leopards, elephants, giraffes – basically anything with a pulse. I have researched how much it would cost and was quoted the following prices from the South African Hunting Legends website: US$35,000 to kill a male lion in his prime, US$13,000 for a buffalo, US$8,500 for a crocodile and US$60,000 for a large elephant. A Vervet monkey can be shot for US$170. Steegh told us that money from hunting helped preserve Namibia's remaining wild places. He said that licenses were issued, and this revenue helped to fund anti-poaching teams and conservation initiatives. This was a hot topic in the press as I wrote this book due to the killing of Cecil, the famous Zimbabwean lion, in 2015 with a crossbow (a crossbow?! Really? Seemingly a gun isn't quite macho enough these days) by a now infamous American dentist. He was shot and then tracked on foot for forty hours before being finished off with a gun. In 2017, his six-year-old son, Xanda, suffered a similar fate.

Cecil was part of a Wildlife Conservation Unit's (WCU) research programme at Oxford University and had been lured out of a wildlife reserve with bait. He was wearing a radio collar when he was killed. Professor David MacDonald of the Oxford WCU reckons that most lions in their study area are shot by trophy hunters, a proportion of these illegally. Quotas are set typically at 0.5–2 % of a local population, but data used to generate figures is provided by countries that may lack the resources or incentives to accurately measure populations. In the Hwange National Park in Zimbabwe, where Cecil was shot, hunters were allowed a quota of sixty male lions every year during the 1990s. Oxford's WCU research indicated that there were only twenty-five males in the area. When this came to light, the government instigated a moratorium on hunting from 2004 to 2008, and the current quota is four to five male lions per year.

I am a conservationist and have an instinctive aversion towards hunting. Or maybe it's a particular sort of wealthy male that I take issue with. Marina Lamprecht, the owner of Hunters Namibia Safaris, said, "Hunt operators are conservationists first, and hunters second." With human pressure on land, there is less tolerance for wildlife. Trophy hunting is the single most lucrative form of commercial farmland use. The trophy hunters pay a day fee and a trophy fee, but the meat remains the property of the community. It's a win/win situation. We also employ nineteen people – that's nineteen families supported by our work – and around 6,000 trophy hunters visit Namibia each year." That is a compelling argument.

Many of the major wildlife and conservation charities are pro or neutral on the topic of trophy hunting. The problem is that any effective quota scheme requires competent managers looking at the long-term future of a species. In many countries, corruption can make it financially lucrative to maximise short-term profit. Hunters might pay bribes to exceed hunting quotas, shoot the wrong species, age, or gender, use illegal methods or hunt without a permit. Illegal poaching grows alongside legal hunting, and the money generated does not always get properly distributed. Namibia's record seemed pretty good compared to Zimbabwe and Tanzania, although poaching still takes place. In wealthy, heavily regulated countries like the USA and Canada, poaching is also an issue.

Kenya was the first African country to introduce [4]a total ban on recreational hunting; it still has a vibrant safari industry worth nearly £500 million. The "hunters are conservationists" argument does not ring true here in the UK. Local wildlife populations are decimated to make way for introduced pheasant and grouse. In Scotland, thousands of mountain hares are culled each year to reduce the spread of disease amongst grouse populations, so that they can then be shot for sport. I find it hard to navigate such a topic with an open mind.

I came away from it all thinking that maybe hunting was a necessary evil in Namibia, but one that would never sit comfortably with me. Any anti-hunting argument can quickly drift into hypocrisy: I eat meat (although less and less these days) and I've been fishing. Some animal lives matter more than others and it isn't always easy to explain why. We could debate this endlessly; the fact is that it makes me feel depressed to know that a lot of people around the world get enjoyment out of killing beautiful and threatened animals in their prime. I think it

---

[4] The Kenyan Government banned trophy hunting in 1977 and the ban remains in place. In 2013 Zambia banned the hunting of lions and other endangered wildcats and Malawi maintained its trophy hunting free status in 2018. Botswana introduced a temporary ban in 2014 to allow wildlife populations to recover.

is uncivilised and unnecessary, and I wish it did not happen. Prince William was in the news in 2016 calling for a halt to rhino hunting in Namibia. A couple of weeks later, he was photographed on a boar hunt.

Steegh's talk left us all feeling rather sombre, and there's only one answer to a sombre feeling on your holidays: Savannah Dry cider. We sat around the fire, boozing and chatting into the small hours. When we went to the ablution block, rumours circulated that a lion had broken through the fence and was prowling around the camp. We were advised to stay silent in our tents, and it crossed my mind that perhaps someone should shoot it.

The next Global Education Conference took place the following year, this time on the west coast around Swakopmund and further south to Luderitz. Josephine and Lynn wanted to come with me but could not afford the time off work, and I once again felt uncomfortable about the opportunities afforded to me and not to them, although not uncomfortable enough to offer up my place to them. Luderitz was an epic trek from Chinchimane: a distance of over 2,000 km, reached through a combination of buses, hikes and shared lifts. This weekend's focus was to look at the history of diamond mining in Namibia and learn about scientific research and conservation projects taking place in the Namib Naukluft National Park. This is one of the oldest deserts in the world and covers nearly 50,000 km^2 (an area larger than Switzerland).

Luderitz has a murky past. In the late 19th century, it was a trading post for whaling, seal hunting, fishing and guano harvesting. There was a thriving port around Robert Harbour where the ominously named Shark Island, or Death Island, was set up as a concentration camp in 1905. In 1904, war had broken out between the Herero people and the German colonial administrators. As many as 3,000 Herero and Nama men, women and children were killed here; estimated numbers killed throughout the war are more like 90,000. This constituted 80% of the Herero population and 50% of the Nama. Terrible atrocities took place on Shark Island; the bodies of some of those killed were transported to Berlin where they were dissected. In 2004, the slaughter of Herero and Nama people that took place during the 1904 to 1907 Herero War was finally recognised as the first genocide of the twentieth century, although the German government have ruled out reparations. A recent film, *Measures of Men*, tells the story and was shown across Namibia in solar powered, outdoor cinemas. Today, a caravan park stands on the site of the death camp, alongside a memorial to the German soldiers who died during the war.

On 14th April 1908, a railway worker called Zacharias Lewala found a sparkling stone while he was shovelling sand. He showed it to his supervisor, a German prospector called August Stauch, who recognised it as a diamond. A diamond rush followed that would see over seven million carats of diamonds produced from the region before the onset of war in 1914. The town of Kolmanskop, 10 km inland from Luderitz, thrived and boasted mansions that would rival any in London or New York at the time, as well as a ballroom, school, casino, ice factory, swimming pool, skittle alley, power station and hospital. The hospital installed the first x-ray machine in southern Africa (possibly in the southern hemisphere), not for medical reasons, but to check for the secretion of stolen diamonds in the false heels of shoes, incised flaps of skin, and various body cavities. At the height of the diamond rush, people were picking up diamonds by the handful, barely buried on the surface of the sand and gravel of long-dried riverbeds. An inevitable bust followed the boom, and Kolmanskop is now a deserted ghost town. It is an eerie, sand-blown place, an abandoned relic from a different time.

My first true love bought me a small pair of diamond stud earrings many years ago, and shortly after our painful and protracted breakup, I lost one. I was taking my jumper off in the Asda carpark in Southport, and it pinged out of my ear and landed somewhere on the ground amongst millions of sparkling bits of glass and stone in the tarmac. I started to search and then began to cry, frantically hunting for my lost gem. A kind lady asked what was wrong and when I explained, she helped me to look. At one point, seven random strangers were scouring Asda carpark, but to no avail.

On another more recent occasion, I had been lounging by the pool at the Chobe Safari Lodge in Botswana when an elderly French lady emerged from the pool distressed and agitated. I don't speak French but got the general gist that she had lost her ring in the pool – an engagement ring, I think. Her husband tried to help, but the water was deep and murky with algae, and it seemed an impossible task. Just then, a heroic young Italian man appeared and dived into the water. He had long dark hair and impossible muscles – a breathtakingly sculpted Adonis. We all watched, mouths slightly open and with great interest; it is possible I might have drooled a little. He kept surfacing, then diving down again and again for a really long time and then, after an age, his hand broke the surface of the pool holding the diamond ring aloft. The poolside spectators broke into a round of applause, and the elderly French couple cried and bought him a bottle of champagne.

We love diamonds, not just for their beauty but for what they represent. In that abandoned, windblown town, I thought about true love and lost love and that single, solitary diamond earring – still the only diamond I own. I felt unexpectedly emotional and needed to be on my own for a while. I was most probably just tired and hungry and due my period. Patricia asked if I was OK, and I said that I had some sand in my contact lenses.

 Somehow Steve, one of the other volunteers, had negotiated a tour inside the headquarters of NamDeb, an amalgamation of DeBeers and the Government of Namibia established in 1994. Security has always been top-notch in this area and remains so even though the land has been processed so repeatedly and thoroughly that only an estimated one carat per hundred tonnes of sediment remains. Over the years, workers have gone to innovative extremes to smuggle diamonds: trained pigeons, shooting arrows with diamonds chiselled into the shaft and swallowing or inserting diamonds into the body. If a guard foiled a plot to steal diamonds, they were given a cut of the value of the loot saved, equivalent to a lottery win. Doug, one of the volunteers, jokingly asked what would happen if we accidentally stepped on a diamond during the tour and transported it out unwittingly in the tread of a shoe. Our guide did not smile. "Minimum jail tariff is set at five years for stealing diamonds. That would apply in such a case." This was delivered in that clipped South African accent that can sound rather menacing. We stopped sniggering and surreptitiously checked the soles of our shoes.

We were lucky to get that tour as travel in the whole area is so heavily regulated. The Sperrgebiet, or Forbidden Territory, stretches for 26,000 km^2 along the Atlantic coast in the west, Orange River in the south, and 100 km inland until 72 km north of Luderitz. It is illegal to set foot in the area without a permit, and most permits are issued only to licensed miners, prospectors and their labourers. Luderitz has had a recent name change, like the Caprivi Strip, and is now to be known as !Nami≠nüs. The ! and ≠ represent the clicks of the Nama language.

There is an eight-minute clip on YouTube explaining how to pronounce it.

From !Nami≠nüs, we travelled north to a research station in the Namib Naukluft Desert National Park. A group of international and Namibian students investigated irrigation systems and catalogued the flora and fauna of the area. It was a beautiful, peaceful place, and I could have stayed there for weeks. The Namib desert is ancient and fills you with awe, I have never seen stars like the ones I saw there. In 2019 a German artist installed six solar powered speakers and an MP3 player at an undisclosed location in the Namib desert to blast out *Africa* by Toto for eternity. I am not sure I approve.

I got a lift to the desert research station with Patricia again in her trusty Volvo (no wrong turns this time), which was sporting a sheet of cardboard over the passenger window in place of glass. It had been smashed by an over-enthusiastic helper when she had locked her keys in the car a couple of days earlier. We were listening to the live recording of *Don't Let the Sun go Down on Me* by George Michael. I was Elton to Patricia's George and had just reached the bit where George says, "... ladies and gentlemen: MR ELTON JOHN," and the crowd goes wild. We liked to sing along to this bit really loudly. This coincided with us arriving at the research station, and we pulled over and finished the song before turning off the engine. We hadn't noticed the welcome committee behind the cardboard window laughing at our rendition. Another discreet entrance.

After such an interesting time at these two Global Education Conferences, I thought it would be fun to host the next one, my final one, up in Katima. We could look at the cultural history of the Zambezi Region. Work was going well; I didn't have a huge amount of time left in my placement, and I was ready for another challenge. The system was that at the end of the last global ed, suggestions would be put forward for the next one and everyone present would vote. I pitched the idea of a trip up to Katima to learn about the role of the chiefs, traditional legal system and Zambezi culture. People loved the idea, and it was voted in. Barbara said she would help with the budget, and Edna volunteered to take responsibility for cooking. We set a date there and then, and I got started as soon as I got home to Katima.

I booked pitches for Friday and Saturday night at the newly opened Namwe Island campsite, owned by the lovely man from the hardware shop. We would spend

Sunday night at Namushasha Lodge before people travelled home on Monday. It could be quite difficult to plan things with precision in Namibia. As discussed earlier, mobile phone reception was poor to non-existent out in the village, and when I finally did make contact, commitments would be vague when I wanted definites. Lynn said I should relax; people would honour their promises and obligations even if I could not contact them in the weeks before the event. Of course, she was right.

The main event of my Global Education Conference was to be a trip to the traditional courthouse or *khuta* in Chinchimane and hopefully a meeting with Chief Mamili of the Mafwe community. This took weeks of careful preparation, following a strict protocol that I had to learn as I went along. Chief Mamili was the *Litunga* or King of the Mafwe people. You cannot just rock up and request a meeting with the king. Months before the conference, I asked Mr Mwilima for some advice about how to secure an audience with the chief. The first step was to get permission from the governor, one Mr Sibalatani. Three mornings a week, he was available for appointments with members of the public. Mrs Mahoto gave me permission to take the morning off school, and I arranged a 9 a.m. meeting. I figured that even if it took an hour (unlikely), now that I had the bakkie I could be back at school at 11 a.m. to teach my late morning classes. I had clearly learnt nothing from my time in Namibia so far.

I was the first person in the waiting room at 9 a.m. and registered my presence with Mr Sibalatani's secretary. Two other women arrived after me; we sat there for about an hour as a steady stream of other people, all women, appeared throughout that time. Shortly after ten, the door to the governor's office opened and one of the waiting women was called in. We could hear raised voices coming from inside, but I could not understand what was being said. After that, three other women were called in, each remaining in his office for about fifteen minutes. I had been waiting for over two hours now and asked the secretary when I was likely to be seen. My understanding was that my appointment had been the first of the day. She said that the governor prioritised appointments according to importance, but no one had asked me the purpose of my visit, so I wondered how this was being done.

I had been told by some white Namibian residents that they occasionally experienced discrimination from Black officials, a collective "now it's your turn" from the establishment. They could be pushed to the back of the queue or given extra bureaucratic hoops to jump through. I had assumed this was paranoid fiction but began to wonder if I was facing it now. I was hot, hungry and annoyed when I was eventually asked to enter the governor's office, over three hours after my arrival, with no real explanation for the delay. What I should have done at this point was remain courteous and accept the situation. I was a visitor and was asking a favour. I had no position of authority. When Mr Sibalatani greeted me and asked me if I was well, I did not respond sensibly. I'm afraid I was brattish and entitled, and said something along the lines of: "I have been waiting for a really long time, over three hours. I should be back at school now teaching my lessons; because of this delay, my classes have gone untaught."

He stood up. "Miss, I need not justify how I spend my time to you but let me explain anyway. I have spent the morning talking to mothers about the money they need to send their children to school. I have been assisting with matters of healthcare provision. All of these are a lot more important than any issue you wish to raise. Now leave my office. I will not talk to you." Shit. I was sent out like a naughty schoolgirl, back into the waiting room where I promptly burst into tears. One of the ladies shushed me and put her arm around my shoulders. I explained what had happened and realised he still didn't know the purpose of my appointment. Yes, of course it was not as important as the mothers and their children, but he didn't actually know that. What was going on?

I calmed down and went to speak to his secretary, to see if there was any chance of another appointment. I waited an extra hour and was finally ushered in for a second time. Mr Sibalatani didn't say anything and did not look up from his paperwork. We sat like that for some minutes. I was determined to be humble and let him make the first move. After about ten minutes, he put down his pen and shuffled his papers before scowling at me and asking what I wanted. I explained that I wished to arrange an appointment to see Chief Mamili. He replied that he did not think I possessed the correct attitude to visit the king. I felt my lip tremble and tried not to cry for the second time that morning. He gave me a speech about respecting his country's rules and that I had no entitlements here.

I listened, staring at the ground, and after about ten minutes, he agreed that I could have an appointment with the chief as long as I paid a fee. Perhaps I should have proffered cash at the start. When I finally got back to school, it was early evening and lessons were over. I went to see Mr Tatelo to explain what had happened, and he roared with laughter. "These men are pompous and like to be the big boss," he said. "At least he agreed. I will accompany you next time, so your temper does not destroy the situation and result in your imprisonment." I overheard him telling Florence the story in the back yard later that night. He told her that I had "gone berserk" and disrespected the governor.

A date was set when I would meet the chief's advisers to arrange the trip. Florence lent me a *shetenga* and a *douk* to wear, and Mr Tatelo and I headed over to the *khuta* one afternoon. I had never been inside the courtyard before and felt nervous in case I broke an unknown protocol. Mr Tatelo and I had to sit on the floor with our legs straight out in front of us; this is a challenge if you lack flexibility, and I could see Mr Tatelo was not comfortable (thank God for my yogalates DVD). I knew that he had a sore and swollen foot at the time, and his little toe had gone yellow; he kept showing it to me and asking for an opinion. Two gentlemen walked in, and we had to awkwardly swing our legs around to kneel down in front of them, shaking their hands using the reverential double hand clasp I had been shown. I caught Mr T wincing, and I worried about his yellow toe.

The men we were talking to were the chief's two main aides, the *indunas*. They were his right-hand men and would report back to him. The meeting was conducted in Silozi with Mr Tatelo acting as translator. They wanted to know how many people would come, what we wanted to talk about and in particular that I would not be writing it up in a book. Apparently, an American journalist had written a disparaging account of village democracy some years before. I answered this question with a truthful no. The idea of writing a book would not come to me for another five years. Word got back to me a week later that the chief would allow our group to visit the *khuta* for a tour, although we would not know whether Chief Mamili himself would be present until the actual day.

People arrived at Namwe Island campsite throughout Friday afternoon for our Zambezi Global Education Conference. Some had travelled over 2,000 km, others from just down the road. We were a cosmopolitan group of Brits, Kenyans, Filipinos, Dutch, Canadians and Ugandans. The dancing group from Katima Combined School performed a fantastic routine to kick things off and Mr Samupwe, the minister for education, welcomed everybody. I was rather startled when the dance was performed topless in the traditional manner; it made many of the members of our party feel uncomfortable.

I had met Mr Samupwe a number of times; he was an impressive man: handsome, intelligent and somewhat aloof – all the ingredients required for me to develop an inappropriate crush. I was absolutely mortified when I had a mental block during my introductory speech to the group and could not remember his surname. Edna had cooked a gorgeous *potjie*, and everyone relaxed and had a drink. It was the rugby World Cup, and a group walked over to Hippo Lodge to watch England play and lose.

The next day we travelled out to Chinchimane to visit the *khuta*. All the men were instructed to wear long trousers and remove hats; the women wrapped *shetengas* around their waists and wore long sleeves. On arrival, we were disappointed to hear that Chief Mamili had been called away on important business, so we would be unable to meet him. However, the *Litunga* (members of the chief's council) would be happy to answer our questions. We sat on hard wooden benches at one end of the building. The three *indunas* faced the group on magnificent carved wooden chairs. The dark wood of their high backs depicted engraved leopards, lions, elephants and other beasts. The largest seat with the most beautiful carvings remained empty, presumably the chief's.

I was invited to sit near the front along the left side of the room to chair the discussion. Mr Tatelo sat next to me to act as a translator, and Addie came too for moral support. Opposite me was a line of older men. They were introduced as wise members of the *Litunga* court; one wizened gent looked to be well into his nineties. I was feeling worried and did not know what to expect, but in the end, it was so much better than I could ever have imagined. After some brief introductions, the guests were invited to ask questions, which can herald an awkward silence, but the group did not let me down. One of the Dutch volunteers kicked off by asking whether women were allowed to be members of the court. It turns out that yes, they could, and by way of proof, a smiling lady was fetched from outside and paraded in front of us. She was the cleaner or *Sabubulal* (sweeper of the *Litunga*'s yard) which perhaps was not the level of membership being questioned.

The next question was from Patricia. "At what age do members of the *Litunga* retire?" At this, there was a roar of laughter from the head honchos who pointed at the ancient man sitting opposite me. The *induna* said, "You are thinking of this old man here, aren't you? When will he stop coming?" Mr Tatelo translated, and the old dude joined in with toothless laughter. Sumitra, a volunteer from India, asked whether lawyers were used when cases were tried here. The answer was no, the chief would be able to tell whether someone was guilty or not from listening to the facts and judging the characters of those involved; lawyers were not necessary. At the end, Sumitra said that she saw wisdom in the methods here. It was as Jesus said in the Bible, conflict should be resolved under one roof by those who are close to the issues and part of the same family of people. The *induna* liked this a lot, and everyone clapped.

Afterwards, it was time for a break. Barbara had made cakes. We passed them around, and there was a wonderful, surreal buzz as we shared our slices of coffee and walnut and lemon drizzle in the ancient courthouse. As we finished off the crumbs, the *induna* asked for quiet and that we all return to our seats. He announced that Chief Mamili had returned from his business and was about to enter the *khuta*. I looked out of the window and saw him striding across the sandy courtyard. Last time I met the chief, he was wearing his jeans and a checked shirt; now he was resplendent in his traditional garments – a blue robe, leopard skin, fur hat, wooden staff and sunglasses. He looked amazing, and a respectful hush spread through the room as he entered. He did not speak but simply took his seat in the centre of the *Litunga* on the large, wooden throne, unsmiling and magnificent.

The main *induna* spoke. "You asked to meet our chief, well here he is. Look at the chief! Look at the chief!" No one spoke. We all looked at him. We were encouraged to take photographs, and then the chief got up and walked out again without saying a word. I do not know if Chief Mamili had been there all along and was just waiting to see how we carried ourselves before deciding whether to grace us with his presence or not, but I am glad that he did. The main *induna* thanked us for coming and then came over to shake my hand and thanked me personally for organising the event. He said, "I pray that you can live forever," which is just about the nicest thing that anyone has ever said to me. I recently became a member of the Mafwe Royal Establishment Facebook page so I can keep up to date with life in the *khuta* and enjoyed a messenger conversation with one of the current members to secure Chief Mamili's permission to use his photograph here and to share this chapter of the book with him.

The chief's visit was the highlight of the conference, and we were all tired and elated when we returned to Namwe Island. I arranged for a speaker from the Namibian Broadcasting Corporation (NBC) to talk to us about rural communication networks. He was called Rupert and worked at the radio station in Katima. He was very interesting, but we were tired, and as we listened, some dozed in the late afternoon sun. Nothing could quite beat the chief, and that night I drifted off to sleep with the sound of hippos in the background and dreams of Chief Mamili asking me to join the *khuta*.

Chief Mamili and the indunas

CHAPTER 13
WILDLIFE

The drive from Windhoek to Katima was long; nearly 1,200 km, and took over eleven hours in a car. It was possible to drive it in one journey, and many did, but we usually broke it with an overnight stop in Rundu. Whenever I rode as a passenger, I spent most of the trip with my forehead against the window, gazing out at the dry grass and shrubs, looking for animals. The first 600 km were through game farm country. Endless miles of fenced-in, predominantly white-owned farmland where kudu, antelopes, gazelle and zebra were farmed for meat. Some kept a wider variety of animals, and people paid a lot of money to hunt them. The farms were vast, covering hundreds of square miles.

This was land originally taken from the Herero people by European settlers. During the apartheid regime, no Black person could live here unless directly employed by a white landowner. They had to carry ID and work permits at all times and could be thrown in prison or even shot if found walking or living on their ancestors' land without the required paperwork. Hundreds of miles of ten-foot-high wire fencing was broken by the occasional sign and winding driveway leading to an advertised hunting lodge or game farm. Occasionally, you would see farm workers dressed in blue overalls mending fences or waiting at the side of the road, but mostly the place seemed deserted. I once saw two businessmen, immaculately dressed with shiny shoes and smart briefcases, in the middle of this featureless landscape, miles from anywhere. It was as if they had been parachuted in to carry out an audit.

Dense bush grew up around the fences, making it difficult to spot any animals. I saw a dead dik-dik (a tiny species of antelope) caught by its feet, hanging upside down from the fence, where it had become stuck as it tried to leap over. The only wild animals that I regularly spotted on this route were troupes of chacma baboons sitting on the verges or warthogs trotting along with their comical tails held aloft. Once I got my eye in, I recognised more birds too – glorious lilac-breasted rollers, bateleur eagles and hornbills.

There was a vehicle checkpoint north of Grootfontein, about halfway through the journey; passports, drivers' licences and occasionally vehicle contents were checked here. This was primarily a veterinary check point designed to control the movement of farm animals throughout the country and thus reduce the spread of disease. A massive fence over 600 miles long stretches right across the country, built in the 1960s by the South African government. This boundary was known as the red line due to its marking in red ink on a map by the German administration of the then South West Africa back in 1911. Historically, it had a far more sinister function. Before Independence, no Black Namibian was allowed to cross the line to the south unless they had proof of employment. People whose families had lived on this land for generations were not allowed to set foot on it without permission. Even now, over thirty years after independence, the line remains controversial. There are no traditional homesteads or villages for miles south of the red line, and the majority of the big, commercial landowners remain white. Individuals north of this line are not allowed to sell livestock outside of Namibia or South Africa, while those in the south can sell their meat anywhere.

The landscape changed instantly and dramatically once you travelled north of the red line. Small mud and thatched houses sprang up at the roadside, and the area was more heavily populated. With a national population of just over two million in an area twice the size of France, 'heavily populated' in Namibia is a relative term. It is beaten only by Mongolia in terms of low population density, one of the many reasons I love it so much.

Stalls appeared at the side of the road selling bundles of firewood, fruit and gourds. Some had the tourist market in mind with carved animals and fantastic looking handmade mechanical toys. Further west was the area of Otjiwarongo, the most densely populated area of Namibia. I asked my friend Besty if there was much wildlife here, and he said only in the Etosha National Park. He said that elsewhere the Oshiwambos had eaten all the animals. It was only really upon entering the Zambezi Strip that human inhabitants dwindled further, and wild animals made themselves completely at home. The Zambezi Region was previously named the Caprivi

Region and is home to only 4% of Namibia's population, made up predominantly of subsistence farmers, eking out a living on the banks of the Zambezi, Kwando, Linyanti and Chobe rivers.

A brief diversion into the history of the Zambezi Strip itself would be timely here. If you look at a map of Namibia, you will see a strange panhandle of land sticking out of the top right-hand corner. It was appropriated by the British at the end of the 19th century and administered as part of the British Protectorate of Bechuanaland (now Botswana). It was a valuable strip of land providing a potential trade route to the coast. Britain soon entered into a dispute with Germany, who had laid claim to the island of Zanzibar around the same time. The dispute was settled in 1890 when, with the characteristic colonial disregard for local people, Britain basically swapped the strip of land for Zanzibar. The Germans named it the Caprivi Strip after the then chancellor Leo von Caprivi. In 2013, the region was renamed the Zambezi Region as part of a national move to eliminate names of colonial administrators from Namibia's maps. I have used the name Zambezi Region in this book although it was named the Caprivi Region when I lived there.

This move wasn't without controversy, as some Caprivians saw it as a political step to remove or dilute their own history. A quick survey of my Zambezi pals on Facebook revealed they were in favour of the new name, although most still refer to themselves as Caprivians. The Zambezi Region has had a rather chequered history and is often associated with rebellion and general lawlessness. The people who live there have more of a shared history with their Zambian neighbours than the rest of Namibia.

Soon after arriving in Katima, I went on a boat trip from Mukusi River Lodge (now long gone after a dispute over land ownership and repeated flooding). We motored upstream and drifted back, sipping cool Windhoek lager and watching the sun gild the mighty Zambezi River. I've watched that sunset many times since and will never, ever tire of it. About halfway into the trip, I caught my first glimpse of hippos – a group of six, nostrils, twitching ears and broad backs breaking the surface of the water. They harrumphed and farted, releasing a fetid aroma, but mostly just ignored us. If you've never heard a hippo harrumph, look it up on YouTube and have a listen; it is a wonderful sound. My friend Addie does a

271

brilliant impression that panicked me on a number of camping trips.

A large male opened his jaws at one point, in a wide yawn. Our guide told us this wasn't a lazy stretch, but rather an aggressive posture to show us his teeth and warn us off. We didn't linger after that. I struggle to articulate the joy I get from seeing wild animals. People in the boat were chatty, but I just watched and wished I could float there until morning. Things only really came alive when the sun went down. It was a huge bonus to my VSO experience to have all of this on my doorstep. Living back in the UK, the occasional glimpse of a badger, deer or otter (I saw these quite regularly from my bedroom window in urban Carlisle on the banks of the River Caldew) is enough to lift my spirits on a gloomy day. When I told my Namibian colleagues about the boat trip, they thought I was mad to actively seek out hippos. They are renowned for being the most dangerous animals in the area, and most people will do all they can to avoid an encounter. Mr Shamwazi told me a tale of two men chased from their *mokoro* and killed just the year before by an angry mother hippo. He shook his head and said that if I insisted on following these things around in a boat, I would be unlikely to survive.

In late October, I joined a VSO couple on a trip to Chobe National Park for the weekend. They were quite a formidable pair, incredibly organised and prone to making me feel inadequate. He was from military stock, and our trip was planned with great precision. I fear I was its weakest link. I left behind some camping essentials and forgot the pin number for my bank card, I felt like their dependent child. Personal politics aside, we had a wonderful trip. We crossed the border into Botswana at Ngoma, where some massive baobabs were growing. I wanted to take a photo for my brother, a huge fan of The Little Prince, but was reminded rather abruptly by a gun-toting border guard that photography was most definitely not allowed.

There was a disease prevention checkpoint where we had to drive the car through a deep trough of disinfectant then stamp our feet over a mat impregnated with the same. We were asked to take any other shoes out of our luggage and treat their soles too. I was wearing a pair of highly inappropriate but rather gorgeous gold-sequined flip flops (I love the Namibian name for flip flops: patter patters). Some of the disinfectant got on my toes and caused a burning sensation. Shortly afterwards, a few of my sparkly sequins lost their lustre and dropped off. It reminded me of the foot and mouth precautions we had in place when I was working down in Devon during the 2001 UK outbreak, although I was mostly shod in wellies during that time. I asked one of the border staff what diseases they were worried about here; I didn't recognise the name of any except anthrax, but I think that would be reason enough to be vigilant. We had been forewarned not to take any meat with us, as it would be confiscated at the border. I found out later that the couple had smuggled across some sausages – I like to imagine in a purpose-built false-bottomed cool box – but it was more prosaically under a jumbled pile of camping gear. I hadn't been told about this in advance, as I think they were rightly worried I would squeal under interrogation.

The drive to the town of Kasane was magical. We took an off-road route through the national park. We saw family groups of elephants, including a tiny calf being shepherded across the track by its mother. Kudu, buffalo, impala, baboons and endless bird life were visible amongst the bushes. We didn't see a single other car on our journey, which made it even more beautiful. We sat for hours just watching elephants go about their daily business. I think a day spent in the company of elephants is always a day well spent.

Late that afternoon, we arrived at the luxurious Chobe Safari Lodge, pricey to book a room but well within our volunteer price range for a camping spot. We pitched our tents right next to a wire fence – the only thing between us and a hippo wallowing in the mud. A fellow camper pointed out a huge croc near the toilet block, thankfully also behind a fence. I wondered whether a few strands of wire were enough to stand between a ferocious, rampaging beast and a tasty human-sized snack.

At sunset, we joined a boat cruise and sipped G&Ts as we chugged down the Chobe River. We were at the tail end of the dry season, and this region was the only reliable source of water for miles around, making it a busy animal meeting point. In addition, the shrubby undergrowth was leafless and mostly dead or dormant. After the rains, this would be dense green bush – still beautiful and teeming with life, but much harder to spot things. An absolute highlight of the trip was seeing a herd of elephants swim across the river. It was incredible; they held their trunks aloft like snorkels and helped the little ones who struggled to swim. We watched for an age, spellbound. I ordered another gin and felt a pang of guilt about my friends and family at home who thought I was being brave, slumming it and helping under privileged children.

The Chobe boat trip became a staple highlight of any holiday when visitors came to stay, and over the years, it got busier and busier. The last time I went, there were eight boats from different lodges and safari companies vying for a prime viewing spot. We still enjoyed it though, apart from an obnoxious English teenager who kept complaining that he was bored. His father gave him an expensive-looking camera to play with, but even with something electronic in his hands he wasn't satisfied for long. It took every ounce of my self-control not to kick him into the crocodile-infested water.

A few months later, I got slightly more adventurous and eschewed the luxurious camping lodges and well-trodden safari routes for something wilder. Jane, Carol and I went for a drive through the Bwabwata National Park that runs either side of the trans-Zambezi highway. I read that Bwabwata means "the sound of bubbling water", but a local guide later told me it refers to the sound you make when you go to the toilet having eaten too much. We were all a little nervous as it was their first off-road trip in a newly acquired jeep, and there was a possibility that we might get stuck and eaten by lions.

There was no mobile phone reception and park wardens only passed through once a week on account of the park's vast size. We left strict instructions with Addie and Babs to alert the Queen and send a rescue mission if we weren't home for tea.

The bush was much denser here, and without a large body of water it didn't attract such high concentrations of animals in one place. You had to be patient to spot anything, and you were unlikely to encounter any other people at all. Jane and Carol had seen a pack of African wild dogs near here, just at the side of the road. This species is one of the rarest carnivores in Africa, with a total population numbering less than 7,000. They receive full protection in Namibia but are heavily persecuted by farmers. I was out of luck that day. We saw some impala and kudu, warthogs and countless birds. Two macabre highlights were a dead elephant and a dead civet. The elephant corpse was almost completely decomposed, and it looked like it should smell. At first, I thought it didn't but then a thick reek rose and became more powerful. Our steps must have disturbed a resting stench. It became too much, and we had to turn away. The bones had been disturbed, probably by hyenas, and the tusks were missing. There was a thick brown coating around the bones that looked sticky; it didn't invite touch in the way that I think white, sun-bleached bones do. I fancied trying to wrestle a molar from its jaw to keep as a souvenir, but we were mindful of anthrax and the probable illegality of such a move.

We stopped in at the National Park office on our way home to report the elephant. They already knew about it, and it was they who had removed its tusks. I asked what they did with them; apparently, all tusks were destroyed to reduce the potential for illegal trade. Poaching for ivory is still a problem in Namibia, but one that is taken seriously by the authorities. We chatted to a wildlife ranger; he told us that he had found a dead civet on his rounds that day and asked if we would be interested in seeing it. A civet is a small striped cat with a pointed otter-like face. They are beautiful but elusive due to their nocturnal behaviour. The warden showed us the corpse. They were unsure why it had died; its body was perfect.

He told us that civets are sought after for their musk, which is harvested by perfume manufacturers. They are farmed in some countries such as Ethiopia and either killed to remove the musk, or it is scraped from the perineal glands of live civets. The latter is preferable these days but still condemned as a cruel practice by groups such as the World Society for the Protection of Animals. I'm not much of a perfume girl but I looked into this, and some companies, most famously Chanel, have been using synthetic musk for years – something to remember if you're not keen on the idea of a poor creature in a cramped cage having its arse scraped every few days just so you can smell fancy. Alternatively, if you like the authenticity of traditional animal musk, why not cut out the middleman and just wipe a civet's bum on your wrist and décolletage before a night out?

After returning alive from our first off-road trip, we got braver still and planned an overnight stay at the remote Nambwa campsite. This was a basic camping spot on the banks of the Kwando River with not so much as a strand of wire or a stick between you and the wildlife. We drove there along a deeply rutted sandy track, encountering a boisterous young bull elephant on the way. He shook his head, trumpeted and made to charge. We screamed, and Carol put her foot down and skidded around a bit, which seemed to do the trick.

We set up camp and went for an explore on foot. Carol had got a new sat nav for her birthday and was walking along, glued to the screen, when she nearly walked straight into an elephant standing across the path. It is amazing how such a vast creature can silently creep up on you. I was trapped on the loo for a spell as one blocked my exit. It was all rather thrilling.

We went for a drive at sunset and saw hundreds of different animals coming down to drink at a bend in the river known as "the horseshoe": kudu, giraffe, baboons and yet more elephants. As it got darker, hippos left the cool sanctuary of the water to graze. This made me very nervous. Lynn and Josephine had told me enough hippo horror stories to make me terrified of them. Apparently, the last thing you should ever do is get between a hippo and the water; with its route to safety cut off, it might panic and attack. We lit a fire back at the camp and drank some cider to settle our nerves before retreating to an early bed. Jane and Carol shared one tent, and I was alone in mine. I lay wide awake, listening to the sounds of the African night.

Soon I could make out the distinct sound of footsteps and the tearing of grass. Hippos! They were grazing right outside my tent. This was soon joined by the gentle breaking of twigs and branches. Elephants! In my dreams, I would enjoy an experience like this, lying unseen in a tent as magnificent creatures grazed around me. In reality, I was absolutely terrified and genuinely thought I might die. What if they panicked and ran amok and trampled on me? The perceived wisdom was that as long as you were quiet, the animals would simply walk around a tent, and no harm would come to any sleeping campers inside. Even lions wouldn't attempt to rip the canvas unless the door was open. Eddie had told me about a German guy who had been camping with the flaps open on a hot night. He was dragged from his tent by a lion and killed. I triple checked that the zip was completely closed, then sat cowering in the corner of my tent, desperate for a pee and convinced that I was going to die. I would've sobbed if I wasn't so terrified to make a noise. What if I sneezed? Or Jane or Carol sneezed? What if an elephant tripped over a guy rope?

Such thoughts kept me occupied until dawn when the animals wandered off. I finally drifted off to sleep until the burning morning sun cooked me, and an overwhelming need to wee woke me up. On emerging, I saw countless footprints and huge piles of dung all around both our tents, many just centimetres away. Jane and Carol hadn't fared much better on the sleep front, and it wasn't long till we packed up and trudged home for a much-needed siesta. Back at school the next day, I regaled the staff room with my adventures, and they told me I was mad and would surely die if I kept up such crazy behaviour.

I had many wonderful safari weekends, but they were always with European friends. Despite constant invitations to share my tent, none of my Namibian friends or colleagues ever joined me. They said that it was madness to camp out through choice. Many had spent their childhood deep in the bush, where it was instilled from a young age to keep clear of wild animals. Crocs, hippos, big cats and elephants were to be respected and feared, not sought out. This made perfect sense, and the few times I had animal encounters outside the safety of a truck or jeep I was pretty terrified too, and it wasn't always the big beasts that caused the greatest unease.

One Sunday afternoon, I stayed at the village for the weekend and was doing my yogalates DVD on the bedroom floor to tone up and achieve inner peace, when a small scorpion scuttled underneath me. "Small ones most deadly" was a mantra that stuck in my head, and I froze. I held my rather awkward bridge pose, terrified to lower my buttocks in case I squashed the scorpion. The village was practically deserted, and my curtains were drawn, so I was daringly doing my exercises wearing nothing but a small pair of pants, deliciously cool, exhilarating and liberating but hopeless at providing any protection from scorpion stings.

Eventually, starting to shake and about to get a cramp, I performed an athletic sideways style commando roll and exposed the scorpion, pincers and tail aloft, in the middle of the floor. I grabbed a glass and secured the beast underneath it, threw some clothes on and ran to Josephine's house, pausing to secure an errant boob that had escaped from my hastily thrown on halter necked top. I thought this had gone unnoticed until eighteen months later when I was due to leave Namibia, and my friends were recounting their fond memories of my arrival in the village. Mr Simataa said he would never forget the vision of me running across the sandy schoolyard with my left breast flying in the wind.

Anyway, Josephine was asleep on the back porch when I arrived, and I woke her up with a garbled shout. "Scorpion alert! Scorpion! I've got a scorpion in my house!" She stared at me for a while, scowling. "What? What on earth are you shouting at me?"

"Scorpion! In my house, what shall I do?"

This went on for some time until Josephine made me spell out what I was trying to say. "Oh, scorpion. I thought you were shouting, 'School pin! School pin!'" I asked her what on earth a school pin was, and she said she didn't know, hence the confusion. I have tried many times since to say scorpion and make it sound like school pin; it never does. Eventually, having established the nature of the emergency, we headed back over to my house, where Joso lifted the glass, stomped on the scorpion and flicked it out of the door. I felt embarrassed for causing such a fuss and didn't much feel like carrying on with the yogalates, all karma and balance having disappeared. Joso and I shared a beer, and she told me about the time she had found a nest of scorpions underneath her mattress and reacted far more calmly than I had. Apparently, 95% of scorpion stings in southern Africa result in nothing more than some localised swelling and pain, but there are a handful of deaths every year, and I have no idea whether the scorpion I found was one of the baddies on account of it being too squashed for accurate ID.

Spiders were another creepy-crawly that could be bad news. Most of the ones I saw were huge, harmless, flat spiders known as picture spiders for their habit of congregating behind any pictures that were hung on the wall. I got quite used to those and never killed them as they helped keep fly numbers down. There were some horrors, though, most notably the straw-coloured sac spiders. Mr Shamwazi once squashed one of these in my garden when we were sitting around having a cup of tea. I wouldn't even have noticed it on the sand. These can cause painful bites containing necrotic venom, which kills body cells.

When my friend Steve came to visit, we took a fishing trip on the Zambezi with two South African men. We drank a vast amount of beer and didn't catch a single fish, but the trip was memorable for two reasons. One guy had a large wound dressing on his leg, and making conversation, I asked what had happened. He peeled back the dressing to expose an angry, weeping sore on his calf, slightly bigger than a fifty pence piece. He said that he had been bitten by a sac spider over two years ago and this was the bite site just starting to improve. Imagine if one bit you on the face! The second reason that trip is branded into my memory is that both men wore incredibly short shorts and sat legs akimbo in the boat, taking it in turns to give us an eyeful of hairy bollock and occasional sweaty penis. Steve and I kept exchanging horrified glances and stifling giggles, but the blokes seemed oblivious. I think if I'd experienced a painful necrotic spider bite, I'd be inclined to keep my tackle safely tucked away.

Snakes could be an issue, too, although I didn't spot any until I'd been living in Chinchimane for nearly eight months. My friend Cath was due to visit, and she has a phobia about snakes; I had assured her that although they were about, the chances of us seeing one were practically zero, and she would be fine, not to worry. With unbelievable timing, snake sightings started coming thick and fast, maybe due to a change in the season as the temperature rose and rain became a distant memory, or maybe just an unfortunate coincidence.

The first happened the night before Cath was due to arrive on the Intercape bus from Windhoek. I was sitting at my desk in the laboratory tidying up some administrative loose ends before the weekend when I reached for a file in the cupboard to my left. A movement glimpsed through the corner of my eye caused me to turn and look: a snake! A small snake, but a snake, nonetheless. My hand was centimetres from its raised head, and I was scared to move in case it struck. I shouted for Mr Chalo in the library next door. "Mr

Chalo, help! Snake!" Taking care to enunciate properly. Silence.

The snake hadn't moved, presumably shitting itself as much as I was. I took a deep breath, pulled my hand away, kicked the cupboard door shut and ran out of the lab to the library to find Mr Chalo listening to the radio and sheepishly eating crisps (no food allowed in the library!). I told him what had happened, and he called for backup in the form of three strapping year 12 lads armed with brooms. We all marched into the lab, where Mr Chalo said we should both stand on the desks to keep out of the way while the boys dealt with the snake. This didn't seem the time to discuss child protection issues, so I hopped onto a desk with Mr C and watched as the boys opened the cupboard with a broom handle and swept out all the contents, including the snake, and proceeded to sweep it towards the door and bash it to death.

I felt sorry that it had been killed and wished we could have released it back into the wild. Mr C said it was a young spitting cobra. Its venom was just as dangerous, but its behaviour was more timid due to its small size. He reckoned an adult would've bitten me. He gave me the rest of his packet of crisps and returned to the library as I set about tidying up the spilt cupboard contents and wiping snake blood off the floor. The student heroes went back to the hostel, telling the story of how they had saved the English lady from a dangerous snake. I had decided to keep this incident from Cath so she wouldn't panic, but we saw two snakes soon after she arrived – a huge cobra disturbed in the long grass by one of the dogs, and another large, unidentified one slithering across the road.

The road to Chinchimane

289

CHAPTER 14
HOLIDAY TIME

I had been living in Chinchimane for less than four months when school broke up for a six-week Christmas break, timed to coincide with ploughing, planting and the start of the rainy season. It was my second six-week holiday in as many months. How fortunate we teachers are at times. There was an end-of-term party in the dining hall where the students sang and danced, and certificates were awarded for effort and attainment. Lynn and Josephine hid bottles of Tafel Lager in the canteen kitchen, kept deliciously ice cold amongst packets of frozen meat. It was clear that some students were surreptitiously boozing as well. One teenage boy, red-eyed and staggering, aimed a punch at Mr Dhlamini and spent the remainder of the evening handcuffed to a metal table, crying, apparently waiting for the police to arrive. I wondered who had brought handcuffs to an end-of-term celebration.

Emboldened by a bottle or two of illicit beer, I practised my Silozi greetings on the school governors, complete with respectful stoop and double-clasp handshake. They howled with laughter, nearly dislocated my shoulder with a full arm shake, and said they were thrilled to have me on board. On the short walk home, I tripped over and Josephine squatted for a pee in the middle of the schoolyard, singing throughout. It reminded me of nights out in Southport when I was doing my A-levels, and I felt quite at home.

The following day school officially ended, and everyone packed up, ready to head back home for the holidays. Combis and bakkies honked and revved at the school gates, and their clashing sound systems created a festival atmosphere. Mr Tatelo was taking Jude back to his village and had offered me a lift to Katima. The staff and students would be returning to their villages, and most would help with preparing homestead fields. Florence told me that everyone had a patch of land for growing maize, millet or sorghum. Those lucky enough to live near the river might grow tomatoes, melons, bananas and mangoes. The whole family would help to get the land ready at this time of year, hacking the hard, dry ground with metal pangas, sowing and irrigating the earth – back-breaking work.

Even those with professional jobs would take leave where possible so that they could contribute. We were surprised to hear that our in-country VSO manager, a well-educated, well-groomed, besuited man called Ehrens Mbamanovandu, would take a month's leave to toil on the farm. Mr Shamwazi (my favourite teacher, partly I think because his moustache put me in mind of Tom Selleck) said it wasn't really a holiday. He would be working harder over these next few weeks than he ever had to in school. Josephine and Lynn would travel to their childhood villages where they would stay with their mums, helping with sowing and planting, looking after the kids, but also trying to have a rest. No one, apart from Mr Kopani the caretaker, would remain on the school site, so I needed to find somewhere else to go.

In town, an incongruous, plastic Christmas tree appeared in the OK Superstore, complete with baubles and tinsel, and I began to feel homesick. I rather hoped I might get an invitation to stay out at someone's homestead, but none were forthcoming; some of the other volunteers had talked about getting together for a Christmas road trip. I spent a restful week at Anita's house, making Christmas cards and packaging up traditional, woven reed baskets from Katima market to post home as gifts, and then I set off to join them. I was twenty-nine years old, due to turn thirty in the next few days, and this was the first Christmas that I had spent away from my family. It was mostly fun, although I think we all wound each other up at times. Christmas wouldn't be Christmas without a few frayed nerves.

Five of us volunteers piled into a car owned by a rather demanding couple. We felt like their recalcitrant children at times. Christmas day was spent in the coastal town of Swakopmund, a Germanic holiday resort blasted by Atlantic winds, one of those places where the beach is permanently slightly chilly but you can still manage a touch of sunburn. We nearly fell foul of puritanical Saturday trading laws that prevented the sale of alcohol after 1 p.m. and would have resulted in a depressingly teetotal Christmas. This rather took me by surprise. Apparently, it was a national law, but one certainly not upheld in rebellious Katima at that time.

We purchased copious amounts of beer and wine in the nick of time. I have hazy memories of someone dressed as Santa in a near-deserted bar, and did someone do a pole dance? Feeling nostalgic, Patricia, Debs and I sought out the town's Catholic Church and attended a packed midnight mass. It was surreal. We sang *O little town of Bethlehem* and *Silent Night* before wandering back along hot, dusty streets to our hostel for the night. The next day we commandeered the kitchen and cooked up a pretty good imitation of Christmas dinner. There was chicken instead of turkey on the menu, and I rustled up some mince pies despite lengthy confusion in the supermarket when searching for mincemeat.

My feeling of homesickness would not shift, and I splashed out on a long telephone conversation with my mum and dad on the hostel payphone. I had been in Namibia long enough for some of the exciting sparkle to wear off, but not long enough to really settle in and make friends out in the village. The thought of staying here for another twenty-four months was daunting. Mum and Dad said they would like to come out to see me in the spring and promised to book some flights. My next school holiday was in April, and I knew I could at least last that long. By early evening, most of us had shared emotional conversations with our families, and as much as I adored my new friends, I wonder whether we were all quietly wishing that we were somewhere else. We drank far too much and fell out over a game of Monopoly. There were tears, and someone was sick in the toilet. Merry Christmas.

I returned to Chinchimane in January and gave some thought to the upcoming family visit. The plan was for my older brother Mark to join Mum and Dad for a three-week tour taking in Etosha, Katima, Chobe and Livingstone. I looked forward to seeing my brother again; he wrote to me every month with updates on life in sunny Salford. My brother keeps hens in the city and in his most recent letter had told me about his two new chickens, Carmel and Mercedes. The chickens were named for the Saints of Carmel and Blessed Mercedes of the Sacred Heart (his cat is called the Venerable Bede). Mysteriously, a couple of months after he got his chickens, two characters appeared in Hollyoaks called Carmel and Mercedes McQueen. I am not a Hollyoaks fan, but when I Googled the sisters, the third search result was *Carmel and Mercedes Have a Mud Fight*. They sound like spirited young ladies. I gather they are both dead now, like the chickens. It is still fodder for family debate: which came first, the chickens or the Hollyoaks sisters?

I told some colleagues that my family would come to visit, and they said they would like to meet them. Mr Simataa had the idea that we should have a celebration event where everyone could get together, meet my family and "give thanks to them". He had rather changed his tune; just weeks before he had complained that I was not doing enough to help him in the science department, and now he wanted to give thanks for my existence? My suspicion was that he wanted to suck up to my mum and dad, hopeful of donations for the laboratory or the church. I tried not to be cynical and told him the plan sounded lovely, and that they would be thrilled to meet him and the rest of the teachers. I was mortified when he announced his proposal during our next staff meeting: that everyone should contribute cash so we could prepare a delicious meal for the school staff and my family and buy my parents a gift. Teachers rolled their eyes, and I could practically hear their disapproval. Ms Mutenda was queen of the pissed-off look, and this one was spectacular. I imagined the conversations: "if Susan wants a celebration, she should fund it herself." In the end, I invited everyone along to meet my family but insisted that we would pay for it ourselves, which was happily agreed upon.

We planned to spend two nights in Chinchimane, and I had booked us into Mr Mutela's house – a spectacular building with a huge, thatched roof, luxurious decoration and a large, walled garden complete with swimming pool. It would not have looked out of place in a well-heeled Devon village, but seemed rather inappropriate in Chinchimane, nestled amongst the mud huts and dilapidated shacks. The pool was empty, sadly, but other than that, it was a palatial lodging.

Mr Mutela had worked for the NBC but was now based in South Africa, returning to his home village once or twice a year. The rest of the time the house stood empty, occasionally put to use for dignitaries visiting Chief Mamili. Mr Mutela was a wealthy, successful man and some distant relation of Precious'. She had given me his telephone number, and when I called, he was very keen to help out. I was yet again struck by the inbuilt privilege I enjoyed. Would a UK TV executive take a call from and open up their house to a visiting Namibian volunteer? Maybe, but unlikely. I asked how much he would charge, and he said he did not know; how much did I think it was worth? I am not a natural haggler and quoted the room rate at Zambezi River Lodge, and he agreed straight away that it was a fair price. Precious said

I paid too much, more than any Namibians who stayed there, and it was not a good deal. I think we got an entire house for the price of a room elsewhere. Mr Mutela and I both felt happy that we had got a bargain. Aren't those the best deals?

I booked accommodation elsewhere for the rest of the trip, hired a car and put together a packed itinerary. My family flew into Windhoek and had a night there before catching a fifteen-seater Air Namibia plane from Windhoek to Katima Mulilo. Josephine came with me to meet them, and we drove over to the tiny airport in the hire car.

Josephine looked amazing that day. She wore a powder blue trouser suit, fitted jacket belted snugly at the waist, slightly flared trousers and tan coloured, stiletto-heeled boots. Her shades were big, her hair was bigger, and there was a retro air of Jackie Brown about the whole look.

As the miniature plane landed, Josephine let out a whoop and broke into a jog across the tarmac, my family ran towards us, and we ran towards them. Everyone embraced like we were in a film, and I felt a huge rush of love and joy at seeing them. This would soon be replaced with the inevitable irritation and mild annoyance that is part of family life, but that can be lovable too.

After a few restful days in Katima, sipping large measures of gin and lounging on the banks of the Zambezi River, we drove out to Chinchimane and took up residence in Mr Mutela's house. I paraded my family around the school grounds like royalty; they sat in on some lessons, shook everybody's hand and waved a lot. The teachers and students were friendly and welcoming; even Ms Mutenda cracked a smile. My Mum videoed everything on a small, handheld camcorder.

We had bought lots of food in Katima and spent one morning preparing a meal for all the teachers. It was hot and sweaty work. We roasted chickens and salty potatoes, boiled pasta and prepared salad, drizzling the leaves with the olive oil and vinegar dressing that I knew Lynn loved. Mark baked a Bakewell tart type desert. The latter was a little drier than planned; it is difficult to cater for so many in an unfamiliar kitchen. When Mr Shamwazi took a few bites, he chewed extravagantly and made exaggerated swallowing motions. He said, "It feels like you might be trying to kill me with this cake you have made." But he said it with his charming grin, and we laughed; to be fair, it was crying out for a big dollop of custard. The atmosphere felt a little awkward, a mix of formality and shyness making people reluctant to chat.

After we had eaten, Mrs Mahoto took charge and instructed us all to sit in a circle in the shade of Mr Mutela's elaborately-carved wooden gazebo. She formally welcomed my family and said some kind words. She then started singing a traditional welcome song, others joined in, and the harmony was beautiful and moving. When the song finished, Mrs Mahoto turned to me and asked if we could sing a welcome song from our culture in return. I could feel my father and brother shifting awkwardly on either side of me, and I looked to Lynn for help. She offered none and, in fact, could barely hide her glee. Ms Mutenda smirked; I bet this was her idea. We are not a musical family, and even if we did have a traditional welcome song in mind, it would not have been rendered well.

There was an uncomfortable pause that risked lengthening into impoliteness when my Mum piped up with a musical greeting that will be familiar to anyone with small children who has watched Mr Tumble's Something Special on CBeebies. It begins like this:

"Hello, hello, how are you? Hello, hello, it's good to see you." Mum has worked with children with special educational needs her whole life and even added a bit of sign language. I could tell by her wobbly voice she was nervous, but she made it to the end, and everyone clapped. I felt a mix of immense pride and slight embarrassment. By the time Mum had finished, some of the tension seemed to ease and after a final round of applause and concluding speech from Mrs M, people separated into smaller groups with drinks and a second helping of food.

We mingled and chatted like in any garden party of new acquaintances. I could hear Josephine asking Mark about his chickens and Dad regaling Mr Tatelo with one of his favourite stories about Art Pickles, the yo-yo champion. True to form, he soon launched into his business idea for producing a condiment called the *Sauce of the Nile,* perhaps believing he would have a prospective market on the African continent.

My parents enjoyed their trip and arranged to visit again the following year. On this second expedition, we ventured further west to the town of Opuwo, regional capital of the Kunene Region and famous as the home of the semi-nomadic Himba people. The women in particular are recognisable by their traditional dress (which consists of not much) and the practice of rubbing *otjize*, a mix of ground ochre, animal fat and ash, into their skin and hair to give it a red mahogany hue. They are immensely photogenic, and any Namibian holiday brochure is likely to carry their iconic image.

I had visited Opuwo previously and loved it. The first time was with my younger brother, Joe. We camped at the luxurious Opuwo Lodge, giving me my first experience of an infinity pool. Joe is an excellent and adventurous cook. He decided we should attempt slow roasted leg of lamb in an earth oven; I think he had seen it on the *Hairy Bikers*.

A visit to the supermarket in Opuwo is an experience; shoppers' attire was evenly split between regular western clothes, colourful and voluminous Herero dresses complete with horn-shaped headdresses, and the simple leather apron of the Himba. It was hard not to stare. A barefoot man or woman clothed only in a short leather skirt and pushing a trolley is an astonishing sight. I enjoyed this display of ancient tradition in a modern setting and avoided the temptation to take a photograph.

Back to the reason for my visit – a leg of lamb. Sheep are not well suited to the Namibian climate, and I could not find lamb on the supermarket shelves. I asked a staff member for help, and after some notable sheep impressions to overcome our language barrier she led me into a cold storage unit around the back of the shop and showed me a row of carcasses hanging up. It is a challenge to identify a skinned and headless animal, but I reckoned on the large being cows (maybe a couple of donkeys), the small, goats, and the medium-sized, most likely sheep, although mutton rather than the lamb our recipe asked for. I nodded, smiled and gave a double thumbs up to the sheep, and the lady produced a small hacksaw. I pointed to a hind leg, and she sawed it off at the pelvis and handed it to me by the hoof. It felt heavy and satisfying to hold, and I liked the idea of walking back to the camp as a successful hunter, wielding the leg like a club. However, I realised the impracticality of digging our earth oven for such a long leg and signed for her to hack off the lower part, which she did with a cleaver in one powerful move.

Meanwhile, back at the camp, Joe and his friend had dug a hole in the sand with a borrowed spade and were burning fragrant *sekelbos* wood in the bottom. We made some deep cuts in the thick layer of fat and rubbed salt and pepper and aromatic herbs into the skin of the mutton. We wrapped it twice in thick aluminium foil, and when the fire had faded to glowing embers; we placed the meat on top, covered it in sand and left it there. We waited hours for the meat to cook; swimming in the infinity pool and drinking beer after beer to pass the time. Now and then, we would place our hands on the earth covering our meal and felt the warmth radiating from beneath. It would be just the spot for a cat to curl up.

Eventually, we carefully dug it out, mouths watering in anticipation. The outer layers of meat were delicious; tender, juicy and full of flavour. We tore pieces off with our fingers and ate them without plates or good manners. Further inside it remained bloody and undercooked, so we got the fire back up and seared those pieces in the *braai* rack. By then, it was late, and we feasted on our roasted mutton with salad, crusty bread and yet more beers by the light of a full Opuwo moon.

We found a chameleon one chilly early morning on that same trip as we rose from our sleeping bags. It was lying in the sand and appeared to be dead. I had seen chameleons before in the bushes by the petrol station in

Katima. Joso said that they bring bad luck, and people are wary of them. Joe detected signs of life in this little one and tucked the lizard down the front of his jumper, warming it up against his hairy belly as we ate our breakfast and took down the tent. He could feel the chameleon making small, scratchy movements, revived by the heat of his body. By this time, the sun had risen, and the day was warm when he placed it back on the ground. The chameleon flexed its legs and made those gorgeous, jerky feints, mimicking a leaf on the breeze. I finished packing up the camping gear, and I remember the plan being that I would drive the car around to the shower block to collect my brother and his friend. Sadly, I wasn't thinking, and I swung the vehicle in too wide an arc, crushing and killing our new chameleon friend. That is a secret I have kept until now.

On the later trip to Opuwo with my parents, we were even more adventurous and headed north of the town to the Kunene River. I read that although a four-wheel-drive vehicle might be more comfortable, a two-wheel would suffice. I had limited funds, so I hired a small Toyota Yaris from Tutwa Travel in Katima, and we set off.

The drive was hot, dusty and barren. We passed through sparse settlements and barely saw any other traffic. Much of southern Namibia is on a vast, high plateau; Windhoek is 1,700 m above sea level. You don't really notice this, although the altitude can cause headaches. North of Opuwo the endlessly straight road suddenly dropped away, and our height became apparent. Below us stretched a mountainous range heading out to Angola. We were on an escarpment plateau of the Baynes Mountain . It was a completely unexpected and awesome aspect, to be gazing down onto mountains.

As usual, I had underestimated the journey time, and dusk was creeping in as we reached the rocky track to Kunene River Lodge. It was stressful and I kept thinking we must have gone wrong. Forks in the track were unmarked, and it looked too rocky and steep for the Yaris. Occasionally, groups of villagers appeared, staring at us without smiling as the light faded. Around this time, my Mum started complaining of stomach pains; she needed to find a toilet.

"Dad, step on it. Mum really needs the loo."

"Shall we stop for a wild wee, love?"

"Err, no, it's more serious than that, Dad."

"By Jove, we might be in trouble then."

In the end, she had to get out and relieve herself at the side of the road in a quickly scratched hollow of sand shielded from the car by a boulder. Shitting by the roadside can never be a noble act, but Mum is a trooper and made the best of a tricky situation. A group of inquisitive Himba children appeared, but I screeched, madly waved them away and they ran off, presumably recognising the international sign for a woman who needs some time to herself. Since that incident, I have watched the film *Bridesmaids*, and am minded of our own experience when Maya Rudolph performs a rather gracious emergency crap on the streets of Manhattan, except Mum had no designer wedding gown to protect her dignity. Happy times.

When we finally made it to Kunene River Lodge, it absolutely felt worth the journey. A medicinal gin and tonic and a calming gaze across the river to Angola, and all was well again. We rested up there for a few nights and took a trip on a boat along the Kunene River, briefly footing on Angolan sand. I could write a whole other book about the trips I took throughout Namibia; it is a wildly beautiful country. You should go and see it for yourself one day.

Occasionally, I ventured across the border into Zambia and made trips further afield to Malawi and Tanzania. One memorable journey was on the TAZARA train. The TAZARA Line, at 1,860km, is the longest single railway line in sub-Saharan Africa and was completed in 1975, two years ahead of schedule. It was funded by Chairman Mao Zedong's government in what remains the largest single foreign-aid project undertaken by China, and at a time when China was strapped for cash itself. There was a drive for socialism across Africa, and the leaders of Tanzania and Zambia (Julius Nyerere and Kenneth Kaunda) wanted to create a trade route from Zambia's central copper belt and agricultural regions to the port of Dar es Salaam that avoided the then white-minority ruled Zimbabwe (Rhodesia at that time) and South Africa. The line was an engineering feat. In the nine months before construction, twelve Chinese surveyors travelled from Dar to Mbeya on foot along the route to align the railway's path. At the height of construction in 1972, 13,500 Chinese workers and 38,500 African workers were employed on the project, and an estimated 160 people died. It was christened the Great Uhuru Railway. *Uhuru* is Swahili for freedom.

If you are interested in railways or the political history of southern Africa at that time I recommend Jamie Monson's book, *Africa's Freedom Railway*. If you feel particularly decadent and adventurous, why not book a ticket from Kapiri Mposhi and read it on the train? You could read it from cover to cover, maybe a few times over, in the time it will take you to reach the end of the line. The journey time is forty-six hours, but the train is notoriously late and incredibly slow; it is absolutely fabulous, nonetheless. Patricia had booked tickets some time ago, and we collected them without incident and waited an hour or so for our departure.

We had booked a four-berth cabin which we shared with some pleasant Dutch medical students. Our narrow, wooden bunks were very close together, but comfortable enough. We padlocked our backpacks to the bedstead as recommended in the Rough Guide and took a stroll down the train. There were over twenty carriages; first class four-berths like ours, second class six-berths and third class seated carriages. We also had use of a lounge and restaurant car. The lounge had faded red velvet sofas, once beautiful carpets and balding chandeliers. I absolutely loved it. We settled on one of the sofas with a game of Bao and watched the fattest rat ever scuttle across the floor. The food in the restaurant was delicious. We had chicken and pap all served on bone china by smartly dressed waiters. There were plenty of tourists on the train alongside businesspeople and families returning home. There was a wonderful atmosphere, particularly as the train slowed to walking pace through small towns and vendors sold fruit, sweets and juice through the windows. We even saw elephants and giraffe as the train rattled through impressive Tanzanian nature reserves.

The only difficulty was the loo. The toilets were OK initially, but as the hours rolled by, they became fuller and fuller. I don't know if the flush just wasn't working properly or whether this was always so. The cubicle window was permanently locked open, so at least there was fresh air in there. I am now going to explain, in possibly too much detail, the difficulties that we encountered. Please skip ahead if you are feeling delicate. In order to use the now full toilet, it was necessary to hover over the bowl, something I am sure we are all familiar with when using unsavoury public toilets. This was particularly important here due to the relentless midden rising up. This was OK for a quick wee but rather difficult for anything more time-consuming, the process made more challenging still by the constant wobbling and leaning of the carriage. Thankfully, a handy rail was fixed to the wall in front so one could assume an appropriate stance, holding tight to the rail.

The other problem was the window – the window fixed permanently wide open on a train that often travelled at walking pace through inhabited areas, where people would gather to proffer items for sale through it. I would like to apologise to the inhabitants of the Morogoro region who may have got an eyeful of my bottom in a less than flattering pose, and in particular a nice lady who offered a small packet of popcorn through the window while I was mid-crap and got a torrent of abuse. Sorry about that. Toilets aside, the journey was wonderful, and we arrived not entirely refreshed but definitely rejuvenated in the spectacular port city of Dar es Salaam.

When I eventually returned from that trip, it was all change in Chinchimane. Electricity had arrived! The source was hydroelectric power from the Zambezi. Solar panels would work a treat, but Lynn said that any time they were installed in remote villages, they soon got stolen. The school buildings, student hostel and most of the teacher accommodation now had power along with the chief's *khuta*. Only three houses had been missed off the connection: the Tatelo's, Mrs Mahoto's and mine (I do not know why). I didn't mind. I could charge my phone at Lynne's and plug the fridge in over there, and I preferred to read by candlelight. Ms Mutenda and Miss Simataa brought great big television sets over from Katima and put them in their bedrooms. We never saw them again outside of the classroom. The photocopier was used incessantly until it ran out of toner, and we started fundraising to buy some computers.

CHAPTER 15
THE MEN IN OUR LIVES

I had a casual boyfriend when I embarked on my Namibian adventure. We were far from being the loves of each other's lives, and things amicably fizzled out when I made plans to move away. I had no intention of actively seeking a new lover, although during long, lonely hours in the village, I regularly indulged in a romantic fantasy where I fell in love with a rugged safari lodge owner and lived out my days brown as a berry, sipping gins and tonics, surrounded by elephants and chattering children.

During one of our many philosophical discussions in the library, Mr Chalo lamented the lack of romance in his own life. I wonder had he been browsing the inexplicably large Jayne Ann Krentz section. He said that Namibian couples he knew were not very demonstrative with their affections; he felt that there was not enough holding hands, greeting one another with a tender embrace and a warm smile or regularly telling one another that they loved them. I imagine most couples who have been together for a long time see demonstrative love fade.

Lynn and Guillermo clearly loved one another. I often caught them kissing or giggling. On nights out, they would dance close together, never taking their eyes off each other. It was beautiful. I could have watched them all evening. I would catch him gazing at Lynn, not quite drooling but close, but then he must have been about twenty years older than her, and she was an absolute stunner, so I'm not surprised. Josephine said Lynn had all the right ingredients for a woman: "big lips, big eyes, big hair, big butt and big breasts, everything else is really small."

Florence and Mr Tatelo appeared to have a rather functional relationship, but they had two small kids and shared one bedroom, so had little choice. Sometimes Mr Tatelo would grab me firmly by the arm and say, "Look, Susan, look at my beautiful wife. Isn't she the most beautiful woman you have ever seen?" He would keep hold of my arm, jiggling it vigorously until I agreed that, yes, she was the most beautiful woman I had ever seen. Florence would shake her head, clearly delighted, and shoo him away. Joso only really ever spoke of her boyfriend, Simataa's Dad, when she needed him to buy them things, thus fitting Mr Chalo's stereotype. She told me that her previous husband had hit her, and she had a low opinion of men in general. I only met Simataa's dad a couple of times, but I liked him. He was very tall, smiled a lot and had incredibly dark skin. Joso described him as the "blackest of Black men," and I never did learn his name; he was always referred to as the Father of Simataa.

Once we were outside chatting, and he was in Joso's house, grinning at us through the window. The room was in shadow, and because his skin was so black, you could not see anything except his gleaming smile, like the Cheshire cat. It was so funny; Joso kept calling people over to look. He stood in the house grinning, and we stood in the yard laughing for ages. Lynn said it was the village cinema. Every now and then, he would close his lips and disappear. We would all cheer when he revealed his beam again.

Some months later, he disappeared off the scene, and Joso stopped talking about him. He still provided for his son but no longer in person. I think we all missed that smile. Joso must have been grumpier than usual for a long period of time because I wrote in my journal, *Josephine has been really rude to me recently, and I wonder what I have done to upset her.* I liked her brusque, assertive manner, but she was starting to push things too far. For weeks she was critical and would say things like, "It's OK for you with all your money," and any time I made a comment about how hot it was or how I was struggling without water, she would say, "Well, why don't you just fly back to England then if it bothers you so much?" It was starting to get me down. Joso had been my first friend in the village, and I counted her as a close friend; I really missed her company. What was going on?

Eventually, I asked Lynn if she had noticed how Joso was treating me and could she think of a reason. Lynn asked if I realised Josephine was four months pregnant. I am unobservant at the best of times, and I think my new life on my own had made me rather self-centred. I was so busy pondering how well I fitted in, what people thought of me and whether I was doing my job properly that I didn't actually spend much time thinking about what was happening in other people's lives and what they had to cope with. I asked Lynn who the father was, and she said that I must really speak to Joso myself.

That weekend I had planned to remain in the village anyway, as it was still a week to go until payday, and I had no money left. There were slim pickings in the fridge, but I could make do, and it certainly wouldn't do me any harm to eat frugally for the weekend. I waited until most of the school staff had driven off to Katima, and with butterflies in my tummy, I walked over and tapped on Joso's window. I could see her lying on the bed, and I knew she could see me. I kept tapping on the glass, and eventually, she opened the window a crack.

I said I knew she was pregnant and that I was sorry I hadn't noticed and could I please come in for a chat. I had made two big mugs of strong coffee with about twenty spoons of sugar in one – just how she liked it – and held them up so she could see. She nodded, which was the first positive signal I had had from her in weeks, and I walked into the cool of her home, not really knowing what to expect. She told me what happened straight away. It felt like she had wanted to for some time. This is Joso's story to tell, not mine, but the upshot was that the father of her unborn child was not Simataa's Dad. Josephine did not seem upset when she told me, more angry than anything. Simataa's Dad still passed on some money for his son, but he refused to speak to her when he heard of the pregnancy. She asked me whether I would go with her on Monday to the clinic, where she was having an HIV test. I said that yes, of course I would. It felt like a reparation.

Over the coming weeks, Josephine told me she was now resigned to the situation and feeling more positive about a new baby, and on 19th August 2006 she gave birth to a chubby, healthy, baby girl. I was away on holiday but met her a few weeks later. I am embarrassed to admit that I had wondered and hoped whether Josephine might name the baby after me (what a vain idiot I am at times). She did not, and the baby was named Lewinsky after Monica Lewinksy, at the request of the baby's father. Lewinsky seemed an odd choice of name, conjuring images of an exploitative presidential affair and a notorious stain. I have just been reading up about her public re-emergence; Monica Lewinsky has made the front cover of *TIME* magazine, graduated with a Master of Science degree, taken a public stand against cyber bullying and delivered a TED talk calling for a more compassionate internet. An inspirational namesake, after all. We shortened it to Lou Lou anyway, and that stuck.

She was the cutest, cuddliest baby, and I took to carrying her around in a papoose where she would curl up and sleep for hours at a time nestled against my sweaty back.

I came across a few endearing tales of courtship over the time I spent in Namibia. One was literally etched into the skin of the delicious mango fruits that grew there. Mangoes grew on the trees in Chinchimane at the beginning of September, in the full throes of the dry season. Baby mangoes emerged from pink-stalked, creamy froths of flowers and were the shape and colour of broad beans. They were hard and furry and pleasingly tactile. Entertainment was in short supply out in the village. I enjoyed standing with the warm sun on my face stroking them. As they grew, the mangoes lost their fuzz, and the skin became tougher and darker. Students would carve their names into the peel, leaving a scar as the fruit developed. By the end of November, when the mango was ripe, the healed wound would identify the person who had claimed it and bore the right to pick it and eat it.

The tree between the hostel and the school building was full of names alongside some lengthier text. "Simasiku is my love", "Simasiku is my diamond" and "Simasiku and Mercy forever together in God's love." If this was a tree back home, it would probably be carved with the ubiquitous adolescent cock'n'balls (in secondary schools the length of the country, whenever the windows steam up, faint ghosts of cock'n'balls sketched into the condensation start to appear).

On a trip to Opuwo, far out to the west of Namibia, I learnt that suitors from the Himba tribe would trek over the remote Kaokoveld mountains to the Skeleton Coast, where they would collect seashells and gift them to a woman they admired. These cowrie shells were a sign not just of desire and love but of great strength and fortitude, as no man could survive that journey on foot if he was not fit and determined. I later heard, via a denim-clad Himba lad at the bar, that just over the first few hills was a shack settlement selling food, beer and an endless supply of cowrie shells. His tale was that the young men would trek out of sight, then hunker down boozing and snoozing for the length of time taken to complete the perilous journey, purchase a handful of cowrie shells then stroll nonchalantly back to their girl with tales of great heroism and no doubt the promise of a shag. I am not sure which story to believe. My heart says the first but my head the latter.

I did not set out to look for romance of my own, but it fell into my life from time to time in a way that did not happen back at home. Charles Luboni (I have changed his name) was a local bad lad, wealthy, enormous and well-travelled (or so he said). I was walking along the dusty, riverside road into town one day when he screeched to a halt beside me in a flash convertible BMW. Top down, music blaring, he asked if I would like a lift. In Namibia, if someone offered you a lift you accepted straight away; I was used to getting into vehicles with complete strangers by now (although they were usually beaten-up old trucks with chickens in them), so with only a moment's hesitation I hopped in. I am not one to have my head turned by a showy car, but my goodness, those soft, leather seats were comfortable, and the gentle purr of the engine was a welcome relief from the clanging hammer of most of the transport I rode in.

Charles was funny, interesting and an outrageous flirt. Despite my suspicion that he was probably a bit of a bastard, by the time he dropped me off at the supermarket, I found myself agreeing to meet him for a drink that evening. Everyone called him a gangster, probably warning enough to walk away. If I needed more warnings, then they were easy to find:

He said he was a diamond smuggler.

Within days of meeting me, he asked me for my bank details so that he could put some money into my account so that I could "buy nice things for myself". (I did not give him my bank details.)

The lovely lady who worked at Zambezi Lodge told me he was a gangster, and I should not get involved with him.

The lovely lady with the facial hair who worked at the phone stall near the Post Office said he was a gangster, and I should not get involved with him.

One time when we were out at night, a group of ladies came over for a chat. They were clearly old friends. They told me they were his cousins. Joso and Lynn said that they were prostitutes.

He asked me to marry him on our third date. (To be fair, marriage proposals in Namibia came thick and fast).

He took to patting me on the head and saying, "Soon, you can give up all of these teaching ideas and move out to my village."

On our third date, he asked me to hand wash his underpants. (I did not).

He admitted to having three children by two different women. He did not see any of these children, and two of them were being raised in a different country. He did not even offer financial support and seemed rather proud of this.

Reading through all of his shortfalls in black and white, I feel ashamed that I ignored every single one. There is no way that I would even encounter a suspected gangster diamond smuggler in my previous life as a mild-mannered, bespectacled science teacher, let alone be asked on a date by one. In my Namibian alternate reality, this seemed like an adventurous great idea. He took me out to the Zambezi Lodge for steak and chips and out to his village to meet his mum. He called me White Sugar and said we would be rich one day and live in a palace. He was full of ridiculous tales, but he made me laugh, and his company was a fun diversion for a while.

After a couple of months, I grew a little tired of his showing off and peacocking around town. The novelty wore off the tall, smuggling tales, and I became rather irritated by him. This coincided with an upcoming trip of his to Hong Kong; he headed off to Windhoek and, bar the occasional amorous text, he disappeared from my life as quickly as he had dropped into it.

Some months later, I was in Windhoek for a couple of days. The Science Fair had ended and my parents were due to arrive at the weekend. Rachael was away but had generously offered her cosy flat where I made myself at home. Most other people I knew seemed to be away too, and I was kicking around looking for something to do. Charles sent me one of his intermittent text messages and said that he was in Windhoek too, and would I like to go out for a drink. I should have said no, but I had no other plans, and we arranged for him to pick me up that evening. He was wearing tight, white trousers and snakeskin shoes with long pointy toes. I thought he looked ridiculous and, as is often the case when we encounter an ex, I wondered what on earth I had ever seen in him. We had a couple of drinks; he showed off about his latest business ventures and all the money he had earned. At one point, he actually took a wad of notes out of his pocket and fanned them in my face. I nodded and smiled and wished I had stayed back at the flat and tucked into Rachael's CSI DVD box set (this was back in 2007 when the original CSI with Gil Grissom was a new and awesome phenomenon to me).

Looking back, I wonder, did I give him mixed messages? Did I imply I wanted to rekindle more than just friendship with him? I don't think so. He tried to kiss me at the end of the evening; I pushed him away and laughingly reminded him we were just friends now. He grinned, shrugged, and offered me a lift home. I thought we were OK. I am an unobservant passenger, and it was a while before I noticed we weren't heading back to the flat, but out towards Khomasdal, a residential district. He put his hand on my thigh, and I pushed it away, still feeling tipsy, light-hearted and reiterating again that we were simply friends. He placed it back, harder this time, gripping my thigh so that it hurt. I realised Charles was not taking me back to the flat, and for the first time, I was worried.

As I write this we are in the throes of the #metoo movement. Women are speaking out about commonplace harassment and abuse. Of course, me too. There must hardly be a woman alive who hasn't experienced some form of sexual fear. For me, it happened that night in a dark part of a foreign city with a man nearly twice my size who I thought was my friend.

I used to relive it every day. Now I can go for many months before shuddering memories sneak in. I have only ever told one other person about what happened that night. Here seems like a good enough platform to share it more widely. Charles started whining about how he had bought me drinks, how I was leading him on, how I really wanted it or else I would not have agreed to go for a drink with him. By now he had stopped the car outside an unlit row of houses, each one surrounded by high concrete walls and metal gates. There were no other souls around.

He licked the side of my face and shoved his tongue in my ear and in my mouth. His breath was sour, and I could taste his last meal. I was repulsed and pushed him away and asked him to take me home. He said I was to come into his house so we could have some fun. I looked around and made out a road sign for Van Eck Strasse. I would call Marie, one of the other volunteers who lived in Windhoek and was at home that weekend. I would ask her to call the police or drive out to Van Eck Strasse if she hadn't heard back from me. I scanned the street for landmarks so I could describe where I was. As if reading my mind, Charles grabbed my mobile, clipped off the back and removed the battery, handing back the now useless phone.

He was over 6 feet tall and must have weighed around 200 lbs. I tried to get the battery back, but he just kept laughing. Looking back, I honestly think he imagined this was just a bit of fun, harmless foreplay even. I tried to stay calm, but my heart was pounding by now, and I was crying. He pulled my top down and started to kiss and bite my breasts. I stared out at the star-bright sky, crying the whole time. He leaned over, putting his full weight on me, and I could hardly breathe. I noticed a small, wooden-handled knife down the side of the car seat, the kind that you might use for peeling vegetables. I grasped its handle, the blade felt blunt, but it was still a knife. In a surreal internal dialogue, I wondered if perhaps I could threaten him with it; perhaps I could stab him. I remember the whole time he was grasping at my jeans, trying to pull them down and grotesquely slobbering all over me, I was running through scenarios in my head.

If I tried to stab him, I was unlikely to do much damage due to the awkward angle and small, blunt blade. Unless I went psycho and stabbed him in the face and eyes. But if he managed to grab the knife off me, I would be way worse off than now. I remember clearly rationalising my different options and concluding that the safest route was probably just to lie there and let him do whatever it was he wanted to do. Around about that time, I heard the screech of tyres, slammed doors and raised voices. I looked out of the window to see a carload of young men pull up about 50 metres away. They were playing loud music and drinking beers. With no rationalising this time, I reached over past Charles's thrusting bulk and pulled the handle to open my passenger door and started to shout for help. I did not know if this would actually help or whether I would end up in worse trouble, but I yelled anyway.

I don't think the youths heard me over the thump of their music, but my actions alarmed Charles. He pressed one hand over my mouth and grabbed at the car door with his other, pushing the lock down. I don't recall his exact words, but he finally grasped that I was not willing to participate. He heaved himself off me, back into the driving seat and rummaged in the glove box for a lighter; we shared a bizarre post-near-coital cigarette, and I imagined myself in a different place. He said I should get out here and walk home. I had no clue where I was and no phone.

I told Charles that my parents were arriving in Windhoek tomorrow and that I would be telling my father what had happened here tonight and that he would be furious and would want to contact the police. My father is a wonderful man and has many great qualities; instilling fear into giant men who live on the wrong side of the law is not one of them. Charles said that the police would not believe him. Everyone knew that we had been a couple, and they would assume we had just had a row. However, the thought of an older, British man going to the police to make a complaint against him seemed to give him pause, and after some minutes, he started the engine and drove back to the apartment. I opened the remote-controlled gate before the car stopped and ran in without turning around.

The following day I met Marie in a bar, we drank a lot, and I recounted the whole event. Marie is broad-minded and wise and was the perfect therapist. I decided that I would not go to the police, primarily because I knew it would be a tortuously drawn-out affair with a slim chance of resolution. Perhaps that was cowardly of me. If he could treat a confident, well-educated woman like this, what did he do to the young girls who hung around him like groupies? Perhaps, he raped them. Charles tried to call me many times over the following few weeks. I let the phone ring, and eventually, he stopped. For some years, I would get an out-of-the-blue email that was friendly and warm in tone, always reminiscing with fondness about our time together and never once referring to his assault on me in his car that night. I have not heard from him in a long time, but I will not forget him.

It wouldn't be fair to end this chapter without pointing out that I worked with many men during my time in Chinchimane and counted them as colleagues and dear friends. I have described an unpleasant encounter here, but please do not think that is indicative of male behaviour throughout the country. I felt safe and listened to and respected by the men that I worked with. The Namibian government has prioritised tackling gender inequality in a way that is largely unparalleled in southern Africa. Women make up nearly 40% of parliamentary seats (higher than in the UK), and gender-based violence, while far from being fully addressed, is at least on the agenda.

CHAPTER 16

HOME TIME

I procrastinated for a long time about whether to extend my contract beyond its twenty-eight months. I had finally found a great group of friends, got used to how things worked and felt like I was having a positive impact at school. I felt at home, and suddenly it was time to go home. I spoke to a couple of other volunteers who had stayed on for an extra year; none of them regretted it. A few had fallen in love and were trying to make Namibia their permanent home.

I met a funny, thoughtful man called Besty (named by his father because he was "the best") and enjoyed my relationship with him, but I knew it wasn't love. I thought about staying on because I wasn't sure I was ready to go home. I was now thirty-two years old, and my only plan was to move back in with my parents and find work as a supply teacher. When most of my UK friends were developing their careers, settled with a partner and some planning babies, this was hardly an enticing option. I didn't want to stay in Namibia forever, and when I thought about my future it was based in the UK, so I suppose any extension was just putting off the inevitable. But if I was doing a good job and enjoying life, why stop now? In the end, I employed a technique I regularly use when faced with important, grown-up and difficult to make decisions: toss a coin. I tossed a coin, and it told me to stay; I felt a bit sick, so I decided it must be time to go home.

It was Lynn's idea to have a farewell function. I had an unused emergency credit card in my stash and decided to go all out and hire a venue, DJ and caterers and give myself a right royal send-off. The first job was to pick a location. Zambezi Lodge was gorgeous but had recently become part of the Protea Hotel chain, along with an associated hike in price. Hippo Lodge, my all-time favourite, had closed for a spell, and the Caprivi River Lodge was run at that time by a self-proclaimed racist. I went there for lunch once, and his response to hearing I was a teacher in Chinchimane was, "I don't know why you bother teaching those Negro kids, they are incapable of learning. You're wasting your time." What do you do when faced with such unashamed bigotry? Looking back, I should have challenged him. I lost my appetite and left. He was a Land Rover enthusiast and advertised a free meal for anyone who drove up in one. I wondered what would happen if a Black person arrived in a Land Rover. It would be such an oxymoron to him I expect his head would explode.

I couldn't hold my leaving do there, so that left Mukuzi River Lodge, overlooking the Zambezi, a short walk from town and with an eclectic mix of clientele – perfect. I was planning to invite around sixty people, and the chef promised to provide a buffet of meat, pap, rice and salads. Lynn said that everyone would need a drink, so I set up a tab to pay for one drink for each guest. After that, I figured they could buy their own at the bar. I put the bill on my credit card and planned to forget all about it until I was earning a wage back in England.

Lillian spoke to her friend Elvis, who agreed to DJ. He had a fantastic collection of music and his own sound system. He could have had one song and a crappy tape recorder – with a name like Elvis, he was always going to get the gig. Everything was sorted and scheduled to take place two weeks before I left.

I typed some invitations and asked Mrs Mahoto if I could print them off at school. Since electricity had arrived in the village, I no longer had to go through the rigmarole of wheeling out the generator every time I wanted to use the computer. I bought a cartridge of coloured ink in town, and one lunchtime I printed off a small picture of my beaming face alongside all of the party details.

Even with electricity, any technical procedure was fraught with problems. I think dust and sand must creep into every appliance and slowly bugger it up. The paper kept jamming, and my laptop would randomly fail to recognise the printer and delete the print job or change the print settings without warning. What had seemed like a simple, pleasant job soon turned immensely stressful after an hour in the breathtaking heat, and I had reached that stage where you hiss, "Fuck!" through gritted teeth and battle to control the urge to throw the ridiculous machine out of the nearest window.

It was at this moment that Precious, the school inspector's secretary, appeared at the door of the library. In a characteristic brusque manner, she announced that the inspector had a meeting at the circuit office and needed to print out some resources. Their printer was broken, so she wanted to use ours. I replied that yes, she could, I just had a few more sheets to print, and then it was all hers. Precious said, no, they needed it straight away, it was an emergency. I silently pointed to the *"Your Bad Planning Is Not My Emergency"* poster on the wall (a wonderful staple in every office), and she tutted and stalked off, only to arrive back fifteen minutes later with the inspector. I could not say no to him so had to abandon my invitations. He said that the laptop belonged to the school, and he could use it as his need was greater. My Mum bought me the laptop and I had planned to give it to Mr Malapo when I left so he could complete the scheme of work we had started together. Right now, I felt like dropping it on the inspector's head. I took a deep breath and left them to it, returning later to find that the ink had run out. Perhaps people could share their invitations.

Another job on my to-do list was selling the bakkie. It was in good nick, although the tyres were a little bald, and I was hoping I could get back pretty much what I'd spent on it in the past year. I still owed my Dad £2,000 and was hoping to meander home via a holiday in

Zanzibar, so I needed some cash. Many departing volunteers sold their jeeps on to the next lot of arriving volunteers, some even securing a deal before the newbies had landed and looked at the vehicle. One unscrupulous couple managed to sell their unreliable, broken-down 4x4 to a Dutch volunteer online who must have got an unpleasant shock when he arrived in Namibia having parted with a few thousand pounds, only to have his engine blow up after a week. *Caveat emptor*, even when you are dealing with volunteers.

I had initially thought the sale would be an easy job as Mr Mwilima, the chairman of the school board, had approached me some time ago and said that he wanted to buy my bakkie. He had the money, and he didn't need the vehicle straight away and was happy for me to keep driving it right up to my departure: it seemed a little too good to be true. In the meantime, a few other people expressed interest, but I told them, no, I had a buyer lined up, and I wouldn't let him down. Lynn said I was daft and should just sell it to the highest bidder, but I liked Mr Mwilima, and I trusted him, so I was committed to selling to him. Knowing how long bank transactions took, I asked Mr Mwilima to meet me a month before I was due to go so that we could make a start on the transfer of money. We had agreed on a price of N$25,000 (about £2,500 at that time) and arranged to meet outside the First National Bank in Katima that Saturday morning, having booked an appointment the week before.

Mr Mwilima was on time and wearing his smart suit; he clearly meant business. We went in and sat down with the bank manager, and I explained that we needed to transfer substantial funds from Mr Mwilima's account into mine. The bank manager asked Mr Mwilima whether the funds were available, and he said that there were some issues, but it would be easy to resolve. "Some issues" was news to me. He then handed me a piece of paper with a long list of names, contact details and sums of money. Some of the contact details were vague, e.g., Mr Ntelamo, John: Okahandja district: N$500. Mr Mwilima said that all of the people on the list owed him money, and if I could collect all of the debts, then the sale of the bakkie could go ahead. I think my jaw literally dropped. A few of the addresses were in Zambia, and one was in Malawi. I looked at the bank manager, who started to laugh. In a few weeks, I was going home. Did Mr M really expect me to travel the continent collecting the debts of "Mr Sinvula: Lusaka, Zambia" and the rest?

I wanted to cry but instead shook my head and said that the deal was off; Mr Mwilima seemed genuinely surprised. I told him I was angry with him and felt cheated, I had turned away other buyers because of him, and now I had only one month to sell the bakkie. He looked nonplussed and asked me to return his list. I suspect that was the only record he had of the money he was owed.

Straight away, I got in touch with Mr Sitali and Morne, who had made offers on the bakkie, but both had recently purchased other vehicles. I made a sign: Bakkie for Sale: Good Condition. N$25,000 ono with my telephone number underneath and sellotaped it in the window. The problem was my truck spent most of the week stuck in the schoolyard in Chinchimane, where the only people who saw it were skint teachers and penniless students. I sent a text to everyone I knew, telling them to spread the word. Jane was tempted, but my bakkie didn't have 4x4 or air-con, and it was pretty rickety; fine for trucking around town and the outlying villages, but you wouldn't really want to drive it to Windhoek or over the border.

A week later, a woman rang and asked to come and look at the truck. In all my time in Namibia, I had never seen a Black woman driving a vehicle around the Zambezi

Region. I wanted to sell it to her just to get the ball rolling. She said I would need to replace all of the tyres before she would consider buying it, and I couldn't afford that. A skinny man came up to me outside the OK Superstore and said he would buy it off me next weekend in cash if I left my camera or maybe a bicycle with him as insurance. I then got completely scammed by another bloke. I feel embarrassed writing about it even now.

A respectable-looking older gent approached me outside the pharmacy and asked whether I would help him out with a business opportunity. Looking back, I wonder whether he had heard from someone that I was short of cash, about to leave the country and looking for a quick sale. He said that his business was selling metal polish. People, particularly over in Zambia, liked to buy his polish for their valuables as it made them shine like gold. He said that I could bulk buy a batch of the polish at a low price, and he would sell it that week on his next trip to Zambia and return the following week to share the profits, which would probably amount to about N$3,000. He said that he was interested in buying the bakkie, and if he could make enough sales in the next fortnight, he would be able to afford it. He showed me a bottle of polish and a shiny necklace, assuring me that the shininess of the latter was produced by the former.

I don't know why I didn't just walk away, maybe he hypnotised me. More likely, I was greedily seduced by the thought of making a quick buck to spend on my hols. Anyway, after listening to his patter, I agreed to give him N$800 and drive him to the market where he would buy the polish, then over to the border crossing to Zambia where I would meet him next week. I withdrew the cash and dropped him off at the entrance to Katima market. He said he would be about ten minutes. After half an hour, it dawned on me that, of course, he wasn't coming back, and I was a complete and utter idiot of the highest order. I thought about the small bottle of polish he had shown me. It seemed familiar. It was a bloody bottle of yellow food colouring with the label taken off.

I ranted and stomped and made endless calls to the mobile number he'd given me. People stared at me. When someone, not him, finally answered it I said that I had tracked this mobile phone and would be coming to find him with the police unless he returned to the market with my money straight away. They hung up. Needless to say, I never saw him again. £80 feels like a lot of money to lose now. Back then, it was over a quarter of my monthly salary. Stupid, stupid, stupid!

With a fortnight to go, I worried I would never sell it. Then Besty said that his uncle was interested. He took it for a test drive, looked at the engine, kicked the tyres a bit while making grunting noises then made me a reasonable offer which I accepted straight away. He said he needed to sort a few things out with the bank and return later that day.

Mr Mwanamwali agreed to buy the bakkie and the money was transferred. He had to give a week's notice to move money from his savings account, and once it had left it would take another fortnight to appear in mine (where on earth was it in those two weeks?). I would be on my way home by then. There was some confusing exchange control that limited how much money could be transferred from my Namibian account to a UK one, and that could only be done by me, in person, at the Katima branch. I had yet another meeting to find out whether I could telephone the bank after the money had arrived and transfer it then. The answer was no, although I couldn't really understand why. In the end, I gave Addie power of attorney over my bank account, and he agreed to sort everything out for me. I trusted him completely and hugely appreciated the efforts he went to. When I finally landed back in the UK, there was a welcome deposit in my cobwebbed UK current account.

I spent a boring, sweaty few days queueing up in various Ministry offices to finalise paperwork. The Ministry of Transport to sign over the bakkie's ownership, the Ministry of Pensions to see if I could reclaim the pension funds I had been paying for the past two years (it took about five hours to find out that no, I couldn't), and the Ministry of Education to have my final reports verified. My favourite was a trip to the Police Station in Katima Mulilo to apply for my Certificate of Good Conduct. This would be required by future employers in the UK to verify that I had accumulated no arrests, citations or criminal record in my time here. I was led deep into the heart of the police station, past occupied lock-up cells and ammunition stores, to an outdoor office in a beautiful courtyard surrounded by flowering bougainvillaea. I had my fingerprints taken by an officer. He told me that they would be sent away and compared to those on file for crimes committed. I don't know whether you've ever had your fingerprints taken; it is a very messy business. When I asked if he had a cloth or some water with which I could wash my hands afterwards, the officer said that sadly no, the water was not running that day due to issues with the pipeline. He offered me a piece of newspaper which succeeded in smearing the ink from my fingertips across my entire hand and adding a little extra ink of its own. He laughed and said (rather inappropriately I thought) that I should rub it on my face to look like a true Namibian.

The day of the farewell function arrived, and the girls helped me to get everything ready. Lynne said I needed a programme of events. I didn't really know what she meant, so I asked her to help me prepare one. Guests would arrive around 5 p.m. They had been instructed to bring their invitations and use these to claim their free drink from behind the bar. That was Josephine's idea to prevent gate crashers and freeloaders. Initially, this was to be a soft drink, but all hell broke loose, and I hastily agreed to booze to avoid a scene.

Speeches would start at 6 p.m. Speeches? The girls were adamant that lots of people would want the opportunity to say a few words about me and that I should also make a speech to formally say goodbye. They said I should invite specific people like Mr Tatelo and Mrs Mahoto to speak in advance so that they could prepare words. Others could take to the stand if they wished to. Lynn reckoned the speeches would last for about two hours. Good Lord. We decided to serve food straight after, as this would be an incentive to keep things brief. Although I had worked most closely with him, I didn't want to ask Mr Simataa to give a speech. He had upset me over the past months and, if I was honest, I didn't really want him at the party at all. All the girls said that would cause problems, and after much persuasion, I sulkily agreed to invite him. In the end, he gave a very sweet speech, and I felt ungrateful and mean.

Lynn had bought a beautiful silver, sequinned dress for the party; she looked like a gorgeous butterfly. She said I could borrow her slinky black dress, the one that I'd had my eye on for a while. I drove round to Josephine's in the morning, and she put rollers in my hair so I could have "big bush hair" for the event. As people started to arrive, I could see that all of the guests had made a real effort to dress up; everybody looked wonderful. Mrs Mahoto was stunning in a gold dress with matching turban. Elvis played some music, and everyone had a drink and milled around, greeting one another. Mr Shamwazi had been appointed Master of Ceremonies, and shortly after 5 p.m., he asked for quiet so that the speeches could begin. I hadn't anticipated this when planning the party, and I was overwhelmed and close to tears when my friends and colleagues started to speak. I imagine this is how a bride must feel, all eyes on her.

Mrs Mahoto said that I had been like a daughter to her and how proud she was of the changes we had made together. Mr Tatelo made everyone laugh when he said that Susan was a Black woman's name, so he knew that we would be kin from the start. So many people stood up and said such kind things, I struggled to keep it together. And there were gifts too – wood carvings, jewellery and a beautiful wall hanging depicting a mother carrying her child on her back. It hangs above my stairs in Cumbria. Mr Pele Pele from Kanono School spoke of how brave he thought I was when he first saw me wobbling along the sandy track to his school and of how worried he was by my bright red face. "It was like you might have a heart attack and die right there in the schoolyard."

Mr Shamwazi's speech was the best; he gave it to me afterwards written on a piece of paper so I wouldn't forget. "We were all worried about how this woman would fit into our small school. And in the end, she was funny and kind and worked hard, and we will miss her. We will especially miss her cakes." I read a short poem about how friends are like the branches of a tree. I can't even remember it now, but it felt right at the time. When the speeches ended, Mr Kambinda picked up his guitar and sang *No Woman, No Cry,* and Mrs Mahoto led me around the dance floor in a gold, shimmery bear hug.

It was all rather too much for me, and when the song ended, I told Lynn I had to go and phone my family. I bought a double vodka, sloped off to the banks of the river and contemplated the last two years. How could I leave this place? I sobbed and fretted about whether I had made the right decision, then panicked as I realised I had been sitting there for some time and a croc may have locked onto my position. What a startling end to my placement that would be. I jumped up, wiped my face and headed back to the party, just in time to see Constance sneaking behind the unattended bar to help herself to another drink.

I spent the days following the party packing the few things I would take home and distributing the rest amongst my friends and colleagues – bedding, pans, crockery, clothes and books. I gave my laptop, and its luminous green carry case to Mr Malapo for the school laboratory, and he promised not to spend the whole day playing patience on it. Jonathan and Jane kindly offered to transport a few things back for me when they visited the UK in a few months; it would provide a good opportunity for us to meet up. Time seemed to drag on a bit at this stage; people kept saying, "We thought you'd gone back to England," or "You are still here Susan, we thought you had left already," and I realised I should have had my farewell party the day before I actually left.

Eventually, the time to leave came around. Patricia had travelled over from Ongwadiva, and we were taking the bus to Livingstone. Besty and Lynn were coming with us for the first part of the trip and had paid for visas to cross the border into Livingstone. Quite a crowd had gathered to wave us off. I was hugged and squeezed and kissed and ushered onto my seat. Eventually, the bus pulled away; a line of colleagues and neighbours; my friends, waved and shouted goodbye. I wondered whether I would ever see them again, and I felt unbearably sad. Two minutes later the bus pulled into the car park of the OK Superstore, where many of my farewell party had just strolled. Most of the passengers traipsed off the bus to stock up on travel snacks. I sat there for twenty minutes, and we continued to half-heartedly wave at each other through the window with fixed grins, shrugging and mouthing our surprise at the slow progress of the bus. A few of them sloped off. It was funny and awkward; none of us really knew what to do, but it was a moment full of love, and it felt like a fitting way to end.

EPILOGUE

Twelve months after I left Namibia, Lynn experienced the worst tragedy. William was killed; his body found on the edge of the Zambezi. Mystery surrounds his death, but the suspicion was that he was killed by a cousin, jealous of the family. He was three years old. William's killer was never brought to justice, but the suspect was found dead himself, face down in the river some years later. Guillermo moved back home to Ecuador, unable to live with the reminders. Lynn stayed; their love could not survive this. Years later she married a wonderful man called Chalo and they have two small boys, similar in age to my own. My parents, Kieran and I went to their wedding, and it was a happy, joyful day.

Mr Joba and Mr Simataa have died too, I would have liked to pay my respects at their funerals.

I miss my friends in Namibia. I have mixed feelings about social media, but it has enabled me to maintain contact with Lynn, Florence, Beatrice, Josephine and Rachel. None of them live in Chinchimane anymore, and Lynn has moved to Windhoek, she likes it there but misses "being barefoot in the village". We have video calls on WhatsApp and she hasn't changed at all. I have been back to visit three times; each time, we make plans to save up so they can fly over here for a holiday. I hope we manage to do it one day, and I hope they are not disappointed. Katima has grown and has more roads, some two-storey buildings and a set of traffic lights these days. The road to Chinchimane has been tarred and a mobile phone mast erected. They tell me the water supply is still erratic.

My most recent visit was in 2018, when I travelled with my husband and our two young sons. We met up with Lynn and her two boys and they played football together. We stayed in Namibia for a month, although I did not visit Chinchimane and Simataa School this time. I would not have known anyone there, and sometimes the past is best left a cherished memory. Mrs Mahoto is approaching retirement and is the headteacher of a large primary school in town and acting as the executive head of three others. I wish our government was willing to bring education volunteers over from other countries to share their skills with us instead of assuming that we must always know best. We could all learn something from Mrs M.

Mr Simataa's daughter is studying medicine in Lusaka, inspired by her stay in hospital as a little girl. I know he would be so proud. Mumbiya is contemplating college to study fashion. We send each other messages on WhatsApp and I am grateful that I can watch them grow up from afar.

Florence Tatelo with my sons 2018

Grace Mahoto with my son 2018

ACKNOWLEDGMENTS

I started writing *Zambezi Reflections* when my second son was born, and it has taken me over ten years to complete. I wrote in snatched minutes and hours between family life and work. I sometimes wish the idea to write a book had come to me during those lonely weekends in Chinchimane, when I was searching for activities to fill the time. Instead, I waited until I had a baby and a toddler and a demanding job.

Thank you, Lynn Kambinda for the read through and suggestions, but more importantly for your friendship and love over the years. Thank you Nansunga Kambinda and Michelle Sililo for the advice and useful information. Florence Tatelo, Josephine Mayumbelo, Rachel Simataa, Beatrice Siambango, Grace Mahoto and Lynn; our time living together and working together has been a wonderful part of my life and I have enjoyed writing about it. I am looking forward to when we can meet again.

Self-publishing a book can be a nerve wracking and lonely process, and I couldn't have done it without help. Thanks to Sarah Gorman for the first read through, edit and words of encouragement. Your positivity pushed me to keep going. I don't think it is stretching it to say that I wouldn't have finished writing *Zambezi Reflections* without your support.

Thank you to Amanda at *Let's Get Booked* for your professional insight, patience, and kind words. Rachael Prest; your opinion has always meant a lot to me. Thank you for your wisdom and advice, it gave me a real boost.

Thank you, Rachel Spelling, for the glorious cover artwork. I know how busy you are, and I am grateful for the time you spent on this. Having one of my oldest and dearest friends contribute to the book feels special and right. James Vincent, thank you for stepping in with your technical wizardry when I was at my wit's end.

Laura Greaves, Cath Rigler and Mel Sugden; your letters and parcels looked after me when I moved to Namibia, and you have encouraged me to finish this book in lots of ways. You are amazing women to have in my life and I would be lost without you.

Thank you to Mum and Dad, you have provided an incredible safety net during all my adventures.

Finally, to Kieran, thank you for creating the time in our busy lives for me to write. I love you with all my heart.

NOTES

CHAPTER ONE

McIntyre, Chris (2004) Namibia the Bradt travel guide. 2nd ed. Bradt Travel Guides.

CHAPTER TWO

Vision 2030

https://www.embnamibia.at/wp-content/uploads/2017/10/Vision-2030.pdf

CHAPTER EIGHT

Dr Guillermo Vanegas

Quantitative study to assess sexual behaviour amongst HAART/PMTCT clients in the Caprivi Region 2006

WHO 2015 HIV goals

https://www.who.int/news-room/fact-sheets/detail/hiv-aids

https://www.maternityworldwide.org/

WHO eradication of smallpox

https://www.who.int/health-topics/smallpox#tab=tab_1

Choice on termination of pregnancy act 1996
https://www.parliament.gov.za/storage/app/media/Proje
ctsAndEvents/womens_month_2015/docs/Act92of1996
.pdf

CHAPTER TEN

List of schools in Namibia
https://en.wikipedia.org/wiki/List_of_schools_in_Nami
bia#:~:text=Namibia%20has%201%2C723%20primary
%20and,them%20private%20and%201%2C604%20go
vernmental.

Sutton Trust and Social Mobility Commission figures
on % of privately educated people in top jobs:

https://www.huffingtonpost.co.uk/entry/most-powerful-
private-school_uk_5d1100c2e4b0a3941866f4fb

Guardian article on fertiliser use:

https://www.theguardian.com/global-
development/2014/dec/05/costly-fertiliser-holds-back-
a-green-revolution-in-africa

Hero's Acre

https://en.wikipedia.org/wiki/Heroes%27_Acre_(Nami
bia) ·

Anna Mungunda

https://en.wikipedia.org/wiki/Anna_Mungunda

CHAPTER ELEVEN

Dr Guillermo Vanegas

Quantitative study to assess sexual behaviour amongst HAART/PMTCT clients in the Caprivi Region 2006

CHAPTER TWELVE

Cheetah Conservation Fund

https://cheetah.org/

Marine Lamprecht http://www.huntinglegends.com/

Professor David MacDonald
https://www.wildcru.org/research/cecil-the-lion/

Buono, "Marc" Autorin Zora del (2011-01-12) Luderitz Namibia: Deutsch Geisteren Sudwest. Spiegel online

CHAPTER THIRTEEN

The 1896 redline – a brief history. Job Shipululo Amupanda. https://www.namibian.com.na

CHAPTER FOURTEEN

Monson, Jamie. (2011) Africa's freedom railway. Indiana University Press.

* 9 7 8 1 7 3 9 9 1 9 3 0 6 *